FANTABULOSA

FANTABULOSA

A Dictionary of Polari and Gay Slang

PAUL BAKER

Continuum
The Tower Building
11 York Road
London SE1 7NX

15 East 26th Street
New York
NY 10010

www.continuumbooks.com

First published 2002 by Continuum
This paperback edition published 2004

British Library Cataloguing-in-Publication Data
A catalogue record for this book is available from the British Library.

ISBN: 0-8264-5961-7 (Hardback)
0-8264-7343-1 (Paperback)

Printed and bound in Great Britain by
MPG Books Ltd, Bodmin, Cornwall

CONTENTS

ACKNOWLEDGEMENTS

Barry Took and Marty Feldman, award winning writers of the enduringly successful BBC radio programme, *Round The Horne,* were initiators of the use of this language in broadcasting, which was voiced by their creations, Julian and Sandy.

Eric Barela, Damien Barr, Lawrence Brennan, R. Chloupek, Joseph E. Cribb, John Galilee, Matt Lippiatt, Tony McEnery, David Raven, Rebecca Scott, Julian Smalley and Jay Yesitsme. *The Natural Bear Classification System* is reproduced with kind permission from Bob Donahue and Jeff Stoner.

The Polari dictionary is adapted from *Polari: The Lost Language of Gay Men,* by the same author, published by Routledge.

PREFACE

Welcome to this Dictionary of Polari and Gay Slang – a glossary of common (and little-known) words and phrases used by gay men and lesbians. Two of the main themes that run across this dictionary are humour and sex, with many of the words showing an ironic, playful attitude towards sexuality, often inspired by the tradition of camp. As well as being funny, gay slang is often subversive, assigning bold new meanings to words that already exist, tackling taboos and laughing in the face of adversity. In terms of academic interest, gay slang can tell us something about the subcultures that have created the words, their preoccupations and the ways that they organize their experiences. In defining concepts that exist outside of the heterosexual remit, gay slang can sometimes be shocking to the uninitiated, frequently comical, but rarely boring. Slang evolves rapidly – words appear, become popular for a while and are then replaced by new ones just as quickly. One of the aims of this dictionary is to chart as many of these words as possible, before they are forgotten.

The book is divided into two sections, the second covers the more general gay slang used in English-speaking countries, while the first part is concerned with Polari – a language variety used by gay men and lesbians in the UK over the past hundred years. Some speakers were so adept at talking in Polari that it sometimes resembled a language in itself rather than a vocabulary. The line between Polari and 'general' gay slang is rather blurred in the cases of some words (many Polari speakers used both forms) and where in doubt I've referred readers to additional entries in different sections of the book.

How were these words collected? For the past six years I made a nuisance of myself by asking gay men and lesbians to tell me their favourite slang words and phrases.

The internet also yielded an abundance of terms – and I spent many an evening lurking on some of the more specialist chat-rooms. Other words came from television and film – *Will and Grace, The Graham Norton Show* and *The Broken Hearts Club* being particularly useful sources. I've talked to gay sailors, drag queens, hustlers and up-and-coming porn models in my search for words – being a lexicographer does have some perks. While most of the words in the dictionary have come from the UK and the USA, a few are more specific to Canada, Australia and South Africa (which has its own form of gay slang called Gayle[1]).

One reason that slang is so popular is that people tend to process and remember slang words better than literal uses of the same words.[2] Slang, being non-standard, gives its users a feeling of exclusivity and secretiveness; as old slang terms are discovered by the media and then relayed to the mainstream, new words must continuously be invented in order to keep ahead of the masses. Slang, in other words, has a lot in common with fashion.

Slang is also creative, and as well as coining a new concept or a new word for an existing concept, it allows the user to demonstrate this creativity. Instead of referring to a man who derives gratification from watching other people as a voyeur, one could call him a *peek freak*, revealing that a little bit of extra effort went into the creation of the term, in order to make the words rhyme. As a group, gay men are often stereotypically associated with areas where creativity is required (the performing arts, the visual arts and the decorative arts) so their linguistic creativity is not surprising.

Gay slang is full of contradictions – it can be a form of aggression or one-upmanship, revealing the user to be quick-witted and giving him or her membership status in the subculture. A single word of gay slang can include

[1] Ken Cage is currently writing a book on Gayle.

[2] Gibbs and Nagaoka (1985).

some people and exclude others. It may tell us about the person under discussion, but it tells us a lot more about the person who uses the slang. It can be witty, catty or scatological. It can protect the innocent who don't understand the meaning of the word, or exploit them by withholding information. Gay slang can simplify the world by reducing it to stereotypes or it can enable us to address its complexity by creating subtle distinctions between related concepts.

Slang contains elements that can be interpreted as humorous or child-like: punning, repetition and sing-song rhyming are sometimes redolent of playground jokes or nursery rhymes. Many slang words are created via tried-and-tested formulae. Rhyming phrases such as *gay spray* and *horny porny* are popular because they are easy to remember, and with a large number of slang items in the lexicon of the gay subculture, it is likely that rhymes are going to stick in people's heads.

While rhymes are one of the most common forms found in gay slang, there are many others; pararhymes (*flip-flop*), repetitions (*fifty-fifty, yoyo*) and blends, which combine the meanings or sounds from two words together (*glamazon, gymbot, homovestite, quaggot*). Alliterations are phrases which begin with the same letter of the alphabet: *happy hips, lipstick lesbian, meat market*; while consonances contain the repetition towards the end of each word in the phrase: *lily of the valley, gender butcher*. Assonances employ a repetition of the central vowel sound: *lesbian bed death, play space, pushy sub, fuck buddy*; and reverse rhymes have an identical initial consonant and vowel sound: *muscle muffin, yum-yuk*.

Another popular method of creating slang terms involves truncating the word to a single syllable (*tats, tache*), or by using an abbreviation format (*ALAWP, APS, JO, MMMB*). The success of such forms of slang can be partly explained by Zipf's Law which states that the shorter a word or phrase, the more likely it is to be found in verbal discourse. Short items are easier to remember than long items, and the process of *chunking*, by reducing longer items to memorable chunks allows them to be retained more easily in memory. Common phrases can be abbreviated to their initials and are easier to say or type. Importantly, abbreviations can save money as well as time – many magazines calculate the price of placing a personal ad by the number of words in the advert – it is cheaper to write 'VWE GWM with GSOH' than 'very well endowed gay white male with good sense of humour'.

A further aspect of using mechanical formations in slang creation is to exclude and confuse outsiders. This is perhaps best demonstrated by the use of abbreviation and acronyms. An outsider, hearing *TBH, LDU* or *MOMD* would find it difficult to decipher their meanings (*To Be Had, Leather Denim Uniform* and *Man Of My Dreams*). As many of these abbreviations are sexual in nature, they give the speakers protection, allowing them to talk privately in public situations. The different ways of creating slang words – rhyming, abbreviating, alliterating, and so on help us to recognize a new word as slang. If we already know *fag hag, nadbag, bean-queen,* and *dikes on spikes,* we will more readily be able to categorize *boy toy* as slang when we hear it for the first time, even if we are unsure of its meaning.

Metaphor is another way in which slang operates. Metaphors are not restricted to gay slang per se; for example, heterosexual men sometimes refer to unattractive women with animal metaphors: *dogs, mooses, horses* etc., while attractive women are compared to food: *honey, sugar, peach.* A slang metaphor may tell us something about the person who is using the word – for example the phrase *a dirty weekend* implies an inverse association between sex and cleanliness. However, there are a number of metaphors which tend to be associated with gay slang, and these help us to understand how gay men and lesbians view their subculture, themselves and each other.

A proportion of gay male slang words contain female

metaphors, a phenomenon with a long historical tradition. The association of gay men with effeminacy still lingers on, suffused with ambivalence in gay subcultures; it can be used as an insult, so an unattractive friend is called *Miss Congeniality*, while a judgemental one is *Judge Judy*. However, other feminizing terms are kinder, demonstrating affectionate relationships – a *sister* is a close friend, while a *mother* is a gay mentor. Masculine slang words on the other hand are used to refer to sex: ergo the phrase *who's your daddy?* Family metaphors can also be looked upon as imposing a system of hierarchical values upon gay subculture, whereby terms such as *daddy* and *mother* indicate power, words like *son* and *baby butch* indicate youth and other terms such as *auntie* or *grandmother* indicate age without power.

Other common gay metaphors involve food (*jam-pot, alley apple, beefcake, fish and chips*), animals (*bear, bitch, bull dyke, bunny fuck, pussy, queen bee*), religion (*born again virgin, having church, hell-sparking the pronoun*), colours (*brown job, black hole, green queen, pink pound*), clothing (*clutch your pearls, flannel shirt dyke, glass closet*), the cinema (*friend of Dorothy, guest star, final girl, zsa-zsa*) and royalty (*dish queen, drag queen, dethroned, the monarchy*).

The choice of particular types of metaphor is not random – some metaphors such as those to do with royalty and the cinema recast the users in more powerful and glamorous spheres. Royalty metaphors often connote social status while the cinema metaphor is a form of adult story telling: you and your friends become the occupants of an exciting alternative world where everyone else is merely an extra or a guest star. Food and animal metaphors are often strongly related to sex, as is religion – sex can be explicitly linked to worship in gay slang, while clothing and colour metaphors hark back to the older stereotype of the creative, fashion-conscious queen.

So what sort of things do gay men and lesbians have slang words for? One of the most common categories are words for different types of people, specifically people who are likely to be encountered within that culture – people are classified according to their age, attractiveness, specific sexual preferences, their sexual availability and how masculine or feminine they are. There are also words for particular places – clubs, cruising grounds, and the home as well as words for outsiders – especially the police, or those who exist on the limits of the subculture – married men, closet cases and straight lads who might be interested given the right circumstances. There are words for specific sexual practices and scenes, and words for parts of the body (especially those that receive a lot of attention during sex). Some terms describe political activism and forms of oppression, while others have been created by the media or by academia.

Slang is one of the most interesting and innovative forms of language use, and this is especially true of gay slang. I hope you enjoy reading this book as much as I enjoyed researching and writing it. And if you learn something new, laugh or raise an eyebrow in the process, then my work is done.

INTRODUCTION TO THE DICTIONARY OF POLARI

> 'Oh vada well the omee-palone ajax who just trolled in – her with the cod lally-drags and the naff riah, dear. She's with the trade your mother charvaed yesterday. Some omees have nanti taste!'

Welcome to a private drinking club in London, England, circa 1955. Men with neatly brushed hair exchange longing looks over their gin and tonics and all eyes dart to the door every time it opens. If you listen carefully, you may hear one of the more camp things exclaim something in Polari – a secret gay vocabulary which enabled gay men and lesbians of the time to indulge in high-octane gossip, bitchiness and cruising, the intensity of which is unlikely to be seen again. While many guys who formed Britain's then gay subculture knew a few words of Polari, it tended to be used most of all by the fiercely camp working-class queens. The ones with names like Fishy Francis and Diamond Lil, who put powder on their cheeks and wore colourful, feminine scarves. They used it with such inventiveness, complexity and frequency that for some it actually began to resemble a real language. Although the more masculine, low-key types may have thrown in a few words of Polari in order to covertly reveal their sexuality to someone they suspected might be 'family', they tended to eschew it. Polari was synonymous with the camp queen. However, fifty years on Polari is practically unknown to gay guys under the age of thirty, and even the surviving older speakers tend to have forgotten many of the words. In the UK Polari has become to gay men what Latin is to Catholics – a dead language.

Polari (also spelt Palari or Palare) has links to several

older slang vocabularies such as Thieves Cant dating back at least to the seventeenth century. It's impossible to pinpoint an exact date when it came into existence. It most likely arose from a type of nineteenth century slang called Parlyaree which was used by fairground and circus people as well as prostitutes, beggars and buskers. These were stigmatized or travelling groups of people who were set apart from the rest of society and had subsequently developed ways of communicating with each other for protection and secrecy. Many of the travelling people worked all over Europe, and as a result a fair number of the old Parlyaree words resemble Italian. The music halls of the nineteenth century eventually replaced these wandering entertainers, and out of music halls developed the tradition of the theatre. Parlyaree was gradually modified into what became Polari, being picked up by gay actors, dancers and chorus boys – who helped to introduce it into London's gay scene.

But there were lots of other influences – the East End of London had its own slang based around rhyming phrases, (e.g., *plates* (*of meat*): feet). There also existed the less well-known back-slang: the practice of saying a word as if it's spelt backwards (*riah*: hair, *ecaf*: face). The East End was full of vibrant communities and so we find bits of Yiddish (*schwartzer*: black man, *schnozzle*: nose) coming into Polari via the Jewish community. The London docks were popular cruising grounds, and gay men would go there to pick up sailors, who had their own slang called Lingua Franca. As a result, elements of this slang also appear in Polari. In later times the language was used by men who worked as stewards and waiters on passenger cruise ships in the Merchant Navy, which have been described as a 'gay paradise' by some sailors, despite the total ban on homosexuality at the time. Words such as *lattie on water* and *trade curtain* were the result of Polari-speaking sea-farers who created new terms. As well as Italian and Yiddish, French and German words, to a lesser extent, gradually found their way into Polari, possibly because they made the speaker appear sophisticated and well-travelled – important qualities when trying to impress the latest bit of trade.

Finally, in World War II we can add some American terms (*butch, cruise*) as gay men befriended and entertained homesick American GIs. Then throw in a few words borrowed from 1960s drug culture (*doobs*: drugs, *randy comedown*: a desire for sex after taking drugs). The result is a complex, constantly changing form of language which appears slightly different to whoever uses it.

In the UK Polari flourished in the repressive 1950s, where the regulation of post-war sexual morality was viewed as a priority, and prosecutions against gay men reached record levels. Under these unpleasant conditions, gay men were subjected to a variety of horrors. As well as facing blackmail and violence from unfriendly members of the public, they also had the threat of public exposure and humiliation, imprisonment, electroshock treatment, or being given hormones that would make them grow breasts. It seemed that the medical and legal professions were obsessed with trying to find newer and sicker ways to punish gay men throughout the 1950s. Because being openly homosexual was dangerous, the need for a language that protected gay men, and at the same time acted as a kind of 'gaydar' by allowing them to recognize others, was extremely useful.

By the 1960s, the political situation had begun to change. Polari was used less to cautiously 'out' yourself, and more for chatting with friends. Its vocabulary – full of words to do with clothing (*lally-drags*: trousers, *ogle-fakes*: spectacles), parts of the body (*thews*: muscles, *luppers*: fingers) and evaluative adjectives (*bona*: good, *cod*: bad), reflects what it was most often used for – gossiping about potential sexual partners with friends, while the target was in earshot. 'Vada that bona omee ajax – the one with nanti riah!' translates to 'Look at that nice man over there – the one with no hair!' Use it in the club, or on the tube – you could spill all of the details about what you got up to last night, without anyone being the wiser.

In the mid to late 1960s a British radio show called *Round The Horne* showcased a pair of screamingly camp comedy characters called Julian and Sandy – two out-of-work actors who were unapologetically, cheerfully gay. The programme went out to a 'family' audience on Sunday afternoons and rather than causing homophobes to choke on their lunches, it was quickly established as the most popular (award-winning) comedy show in the country, attracting about 9 million listeners a week.

And every week, thanks to Polari, Jules and Sand made a mockery of the BBC's censors. This was mainly due to their use of Polari and innuendo to disguise much of what they were talking about. When Sandy enthused about some man's bulging lallies or complained about the rough trade he'd been having lately, it was done in a subtle, clever way that escaped the attention of the censors and 'Disgusted from Tunbridge Wells'. In one episode, they are domestic helps and have been shown into a kitchen where they are expected to get to work. 'I can't work in here,' complains Julian. 'All the dishes are dirty!' 'Ooh speak for yourself, ducky!' retorts Sandy. This is a clever triple innuendo. The audience would probably get the use of the word *dish* as an attractive young man, as in 'isn't he dishy?', but well-versed Polari speakers also know that *dish* means anus, which would afford them an extra special laugh.

Julian and Sandy were subversive in other ways too. At a time when many of the other fictional representations of gay men and lesbians in the media ended up by dying in the final scene, this cheerfully unapologetic pair of queens made for a refreshing change. Young gay guys living in the middle of nowhere heard Julian and Sandy and were given hope – they were no longer alone.

However, in the 1970s, Polari started to fade from people's memories. Julian and Sandy had represented a swan-song of sorts in any case. In 1967 (the same year that *Round the Horne* was at its peak, winning the award for best comedy radio programme), the legal situation for the average gay man was improved with the implementation of the Wolfenden Report's recommendations of ten years earlier. Homosexuality was partially decriminalized (although there were still a variety of ways that men could be prosecuted for having gay sex), and as a result, there was less of a need for a secret language. In addition to that, Julian and Sandy gave Polari a kind of doomed respectability – they had inadvertently blurted out the secret via the radio every week. What was the point of using Polari when Aunt Beryl listened to *Round The Horne* and was able to get the gist of what you were saying?

And ultimately, there were political reasons for ditching Polari – it was associated with oppression, and the early Gay Liberationists wanted to put all of that behind them. It was easy to criticize Polari as being sexist, racist and brimming over with internalized homophobia. Gay magazines of the early 1970s are quick to cast Polari as keeping gay men in a ghetto. One writer warns that gay culture is going to become consumed by a 'language of body parts and fucking'. This was the era when John Inman, who played camp Mr Humphries in the British sitcom *Are You Being Served?*, was picketed outside Brighton's Dome Hall by gay men for 'contributing to the television distortion of the image of homosexuals'. Gay men wanted a new image in order to counter decades of 'sissy jibes'. Anything connected to camp was eschewed.

So by the beginning of the 1980s, Polari had all but vanished from the UK gay scene, and in place of the fey Polari speakers were American influences – butch was in, and the Marlboro Man look – muscles, leather, denim, facial hair, uniforms, boots etc., became fashionable. The *clone* look was discovered, and with minor modifications still exists today. Suddenly going to the gym became a popular pastime and the gay scene was in danger of becoming populated with butch Marys who took their masculinity and muscle tone ever so seriously. Butch gay men aren't supposed to speak Polari – instead they grunt and show you a coloured handkerchief so that you know what they're into.

However, as the 1990s progressed, the situation changed again. With more people becoming relaxed about sexuality, Polari has recently undergone a revival of interest. It's now possible to view it as part of gay heritage – a weapon that was used to fight oppression, and something that gay men can be proud of again. Camp is no longer viewed as apolitical – for example, the London branch of the Sisters of Perpetual Indulgence use 'High Polari' in their blessings, sermons and canonizations – adding a bit of religious mystique whilst also acknowledging gay history within their ceremonies. In some London hotspots you'll overhear Klub Polari being spoken, a mix of Techno/Indie Club slang with bits of East London and Asian dialects thrown in. There's also been academic interest in the language – Polari is now recast as an important aspect of gay social history as well as being linguistically interesting. That little bit of historic distance has allowed Polari to be seen under kinder lighting conditions. And anyone who wants to add some authentic mid-twentieth century atmosphere in their film, book or play or pop song about gay men can drop a few words of Polari into their script for instant credibility (see *Love Is The Devil, The Velvet Goldmine* or Morrissey's *Piccadilly Palare* for examples). Polari has become a signifier to represent being British and gay in the 1950s or 1960s in the same way that platform shoes or a space-hopper represent the 1970s.

However, Polari still occupies a controversial position in the hearts of contemporary gay men. In 1999 *Boyz* magazine ran a telephone debate on Polari over several issues, unearthing a number of conflicting attitudes about it. Some callers were quick to dismiss Polari as camp nonsense, only spoken by unfashionable people who lived 'in the sticks' (i.e. outside London). Such words are 'neither useful, relevant or reflect the queer society we live in today,' complained one caller. Others argued that it was harmless fun, and to ignore Polari is to do an injustice to the men and women who lived through more oppressive times. *Boyz* joined in, labelling Polari as 'evil', with its tongue placed firmly in its cheek.

It's unlikely that Polari will ever be revived to the extent that it was used in the 1950s – but that's no shame. Without realizing it, many of the words that people consider to be 'gay slang' were once part of Polari's lexicon – *chicken, trade, butch, camp, cottage* etc. These words, which are more useful in describing gay experiences because they don't have heterosexual equivalents, have survived while other words like *nanna*: awful, *poll*: wig, *order*: go etc., have fallen into disuse. That's not to say that it can't be fun to use them occasionally. Speaking a few words of Polari is hardly going to cause your wrist to go limp. And in any case, little bits of Polari have even been incorporated into mainstream slang. For example – the word *naff* was originally used as a Polari acronym meaning 'Not Available For Fucking'. Now it simply refers to something that's tasteless. Most likely it was overheard by heterosexuals – 'oh don't bother with him, he's naff!', inferred to mean something bad, and crossed over into mainstream slang, the new users not realizing that the word was originally an insult used on them.

So while it's important that a situation should never arise where gay men and lesbians need to use a secret language again, we do ourselves no favours by distancing ourselves completely from Polari. From the initial 1960s media representations of effeminate, camp queens, through to the hyper-masculine alternatives created by the gay subculture in the 1970s, the recent years have seen a resurgence and a reappraisal of both identities. Distinctions between the two, however, are now more blurred than ever. Polari, as a form of camp humour, protection and attack, is worth remembering – a gay 'language' which serves as a testament to those who lived through times very different to our own.

DICTIONARY OF POLARI

INTRODUCTORY NOTE

It is unlikely that any Polari speaker would have used or even known all of the words listed in this section. A Polari word will possess multiple spellings, meanings, origins and in some cases pronunciations, due to the secretive, unstandardized, constantly-changing nature of the lexicon. Where I have made an 'educated guess' as to the origin of a word or phrase, or have been unsure of the credibility of the source, I have noted this in the entry with the word 'possible' or 'possibly'.

Each word is presented in the following order, though not all these categories are covered in every case:

The word, plus alternative spellings. Phonetic pronunciation. Grammatical category. Meaning(s). Etymology. Other notes. Examples of use. Related words.

See **Main Entry** refers the reader to an alternative or fuller definition in the Dictionary of Gay Slang.

As Polari was a spoken language variety first and foremost, attempts to write it down have generally been phonetic. The following pronunciation guide should be useful in interpreting the phonetic spelling of each word:

Consonants		Vowels	
b	**b**all	iː	sh**ee**p
d	**d**raw	i	bus**y**
dʒ	ju**dge**	ɪ	sh**i**p
f	**f**all	e	l**e**t
g	**g**ive	æ	b**a**t
h	**h**elp	ɑː	h**ea**rt
j	**y**es	ɒ	c**o**d

k	cold kite
l	like tall
m	man
n	nice
ŋ	thing
p	pin
r	ring
s	sit
ʃ	shoot
t	to
tʃ	cheat
θ	thing
ð	then
v	vow
z	zoo
ʒ	measure

ɔ:	ball
ʊ	bush
ʌ	shut
u:	boot
ɜ:	bird
ə	colour the
eɪ	make
aɪ	bite
ɔɪ	boy
əʊ	note
aʊ	crowd
ɪə	here
eə	there
ʊə	poor

NUMBERS

½	medza
1	una, oney
2	dooey
3	tray
4	quarter
5	chinker
6	say
7	say oney, setter
8	say dooey, otter
9	say tray, nobber
10	daiture
11	long dedger, lepta
12	kenza

A

AC/DC /eɪ si: di: si:/ 1. noun: a couple. 2. adjective: bisexual.

acting dickey /æktɪŋ dɪki/ noun: temporary work.

active /æktɪv/ adjective: butch or bull in trade.

affair, affaire /ə'feə/ noun: someone with whom a (usually same-sex) sexual/emotional relationship is shared, of any length of time i.e. ten minutes to ten years. From French.

ajax /eɪdʒkz/ preposition: nearby. Perhaps from a truncation of the English *adjacent.*

alamo /æləməʊ/ vocative: 'I'm hot for you'. Derived from the acronym for *Lick Me Out* (LMO).

almond rocks /'ɑ:mənd rɒks/ noun: socks. From Cockney rhyming slang.

and no flies /ənd nəʊ flaɪz/ vocative: honestly! I'm telling the truth! Also *and no mogue?*

antique HP /æn'ti:k eɪtʃ pi/ noun: old gay man (the *HP* part stands for *homee palone*).

aqua, acqua /ækwə/ noun: water. from Parlyaree via Italian *acqua.*

aris /'ærɪs/ noun: arse, via a chain of Cockney Rhyming Slang and Parlyaree. From 'arse' we get 'bottle and glass'

From 'bottle' we get 'aristotle', and from 'aristotle' we get 'aris'.

> Sandy: Oh, anything else Jules?
> Julian: One moth-eaten Shetland tweed. Ooh! Look, he's got a baggy old aris!
> Sandy: I'll say he has.
>
> Bona Rags

arva, harva /ɑːvə/ verb: sexual intercourse. Probably a truncation of *charva* from Parlyaree. Also noun e.g. *to have the arva*. Anal intercourse was referred to as *'the full harva'*.

aspro, aspra /æsprəʊ/ noun: a prostitute, from Parlyaree via truncation of English *arse pro(stitute).*

auntie /ˈɑːnti/ noun: an older gay man.

aunt nell /ˈɑːnt nel/ 1. verb: to listen. 2. imperative: be quiet!

aunt nells /ˈɑːnt nelz/ noun: ears.

aunt nelly fakes /ˈɑːnt neli feɪks/ noun: earrings.

B

B-flat omee /biː flæt əʊmi/ noun: a fat man. From rhyming slang.

back slums /bæk slʊmz/ noun: back-rooms or dark-rooms in gay bars or bath-houses where sex occurs, originally the term referred to gambling dens or a district where the houses and conditions of life were of a 'wretched character'.

badge cove /ˈbædʒ kəʊv/ noun: an old person. From Cant.

bagaga, bagadga /bæˈgædʒə/ noun: a penis. From Italian *bagaggio*: baggage?

balony, balonie /ˈbəˈləʊni/ noun: rubbish. Possibly from bolonga (sausage). US slang.

barkey, barkie, barky /ˈbɑːki/ noun: a sailor, from Italian *barca*: boat? First recorded early eighteenth century.

barnet /ˈbɑːnɪt/ noun: hair. From nineteenth century Cockney Rhyming Slang – Barnet Fair.

> Julian: You got your blue rinse, you got your grey rinse, you can have any colour to match your barnet.
>
> Bona Pets

barney /ˈbɑːni/ noun: a fight.

bat, batts, bates /bæts/ /beɪts/ 1. noun: a shoe. 2. verb: shuffle or dance on-stage.

batter /ˈbætə/ noun: prostitution. To go *on the batter* was to walk the streets as a prostitute.

battery /ˈbætəri/ verb: to knock down. From Italian: *battere*.

battyfang /ˈbætɪfæŋ/ verb: to hit and bite.

beak /biːk/ noun: a magistrate. From Pedlar's French.

beancove /biːn kəʊv/ noun: a young person. From Cant.

bedroom /'bedru:m/ noun: any place where men can have sex. Generally used to refer to a toilet cubicle in a **cottage**, but can also apply to lock-up 'rest-rooms' in saunas.

beef curtains /bi:f 'kɜ:tɪnz/ noun: 'flaps' on a woman's vagina.

ben, bene /bene/ adjective: good. From Italian: *bene.*

benar /benɑ:/ adjective: better.

bencove /benkəʊv/ noun: a friend. From the Cant *bene-cove,* literally a good fellow.

betty bracelets /'beti 'breɪslətz/ noun: police.

bevvy, beverada, bevie, bevois /bevi/ 1. noun: a drink (especially beer). 2. noun: a public house. Survived into common slang usage. Also *bevvied* (to be drunk). From Italian: *bev.*

bevvy omee /bevi əʊmi/ noun: a drunkard.

bexleys /beksli:z/ noun: teeth. From Cockney rhyming slang: Bexley Heath.

bianc, beyonek, beone, beyong /bi:jəuni/ noun: a shilling. From Parlyaree.

bibi /bibi/ adjective: bisexual.

bijou /bi:ʒu:/ adjective: small. From French. Although *bijou* means *small,* it is also used to indicate a positive evaluation towards something – small is good e.g. *I've got a bona bijou flatette just up the road from Shepherd's Bush.* An earlier meaning of *bijou,* dating around the thirteenth century, means finger-ring, and can also be applied to any kind of jewel, trinket or gem.

billingsgate /'bɪlɪŋsgeɪt/ noun: bad language. The proper name (presumably from a personal name *Billing*) of one of the gates of London, and hence of the fish-market there established. The seventeenth century references to the 'rhetoric' or abusive language of this market are frequent, and hence foul language is itself called 'billingsgate'.

billy doo /bɪli du:/ noun: love letter. Derived from the French *billet doux.*

bimbo /'bɪmbəʊ/ noun: a dupe.

bimph /bɪmf/ noun: toilet paper.

binco /'bɪnkəʊ/ noun: a kerosine flare. From Italian: *binco* (white).

bins /bɪnz/ noun: spectacles.

bit of hard /bɪt əv hɑ:d/ noun: sexual partner (male), especially *trade.*

bitaine /bɪteɪn/ noun: a prostitute.

bitch /bɪtʃ/ see **Main Entry**.

blag /blæg/ verb: to make a sexual pick-up.

blazé queen /blɑ:zeɪ kwi:n/ noun: used to describe an 'up-market' homosexual.

blocked /blɒkd/ adjective: to be high on drugs. From 1960s drug-user's slang.

blow /bləʊ/ verb: to give oral sex. Truncated version of *blow-job* from US slang.

BMQ /bi em kju:/ noun: acronym for *Black Market Queen* – someone who hides his homosexuality.

bod /bɒd/ noun: body.

bodega /bɒd'eɪdʒə/ noun: a shop. From Spanish.

bold /bəʊld/ adjective: 1. *bold* has a meaning specific to *Round the Horne*, which is used to mark reference to homosexuality. Whenever Mr Horne interprets a double entendre in its rude sense, or when he uses Polari himself, Julian and Sandy immediately label him as bold:

> Sandy: Would you like us to lay on a turkey?
> Kenneth Horne: Well I hadn't planned on a cabaret.
> Sandy: Oh he's bold!
>
> Bona Caterers

As well as meaning brave, fearless and stout-hearted, the *Oxford English Dictionary* (1994) lists a secondary meaning of *bold*; an audacious or shameless person, which is perhaps associated with the meaning which Julian and Sandy had in mind. Because of the need to keep references to homosexuality hidden, only the brave, or careless would dare to use the euphemisms and innuendoes which would reveal their true natures. To be bold, in the Julian and Sandy sense, is to be homosexual. Even to use the word *bold* is to be linked to homosexuality, as it shows an understanding of a subtext which would not be available otherwise.

2. *Bold* could also be used to imply that someone wasn't very pleasant, e.g. *bold palone of the latty* when the landlady wasn't being very co-operative.

bolus /ˈbəʊləs/ noun: a chemist. Originally a seventeenth century word referring to any form of medicine that came as a rounded pill.

bona /ˈbəʊnə/ 1. adjective: good.

Julian: How bona to vada your dolly old eke.
Bona School of Languages

2. adverb: well.

Julian: Order lau your luppers on the strillers bona.
Bona Guesthouse

From Italian: *buono*, Lihgua Franca: *bona*.

bona nochy /ˈbəʊnə nɒʃti/ vocative: good night.

bona vardering /ˈbəʊnə vɑːdərɪŋ/ adjective: attractive. Literally 'good looking'.

(the) bones /bəʊnz/ noun: one's boyfriend.

boobs /buːbz/ noun: breasts. Originally US slang.

booth /ˈbuːð/ noun: a room, especially a bedroom.

box /bɒks/ noun: posterior.

boyno /bɔɪnəʊ/ vocative: hello.

brads /brædz/ noun: money. From Cant.

brainless /ˈbreɪnləs/ adjective: good.

brandy /brændi/ noun: posterior. From Cockney rhyming slang 'brandy and rum' = bum.

brandy latch /brændi lætʃ/ noun: a toilet (lock-up).

bugle /bju:gəl/ noun: a nose. Originally used to refer to buffalo or oxen, the term occurs in connection with military instruments of brass or copper used as signal-horns for the infantry. To be 'bugle-browed' is to have horns like a wild ox. The connection of *bugle* with the nose may be to do with the shape of the nose, or the noise it makes.

bull /bʊl/ noun: a masculine female.

butch /bʊtʃ/ See **Main Entry**.

buvare /bju:'vɑ:reɪ/ noun: something drinkable. From French *buv* – stem of boire: to drink.

C

cabouche /kə'bu:ʃ/ noun: a car. Derived from *caboose* which was originally eighteenth century Navy slang referring to the kitchen of merchantmen on deck. By the nineteenth century the word was used in the US to refer to a van or car on a freight train. By the early twentieth century the Canadian usage of the word referred to a mobile hut or bunk-house, moved on wheels or runners.

cackle /'kækəl/ noun: talk. From seventeenth century slang: 'cut the cackle'.

cackling fart /kæklɪŋ fɑ:t/ noun: egg. From Cant.

camisa, commision, mish /kæmi:sə/ noun: a shirt. Parlyaree. Seventeenth century. Derived from the Italian *camicia*.

camp /kæmp/ See **Main Entry**.

capella, capolla, capelli, kapella /kæ'pelə/ noun: a hat or cap. Parlyaree via Italian.

carnish /kɑ:nɪʃ/ noun: meat, food. From Italian: *Carne.*

carnish ken /kɑ:nɪʃ ken/ noun: an eating house.

caroon /kəru:n/ noun: crown piece.

carsey, karsey /kɑ:si/ 1. noun: house. 2. noun: toilet. 3. noun: brothel. From Italian: *casa.*

cartes /kɑ:ts/ noun: a penis.

cartzo /kɑ:tzəʊ/ noun: a penis. From Italian: *cazzo* (thrust).

catever, kerterver /kætevə/ adjective: bad. Parlyaree. Via Italian: Cattivo.

cats /kætz/ noun: trousers.

cavaliers and roundheads /kævə'lɪəz ən raʊndhedz/ noun: uncircumcized and circumcised penises.

caxton /kækztən/ noun: a wig.

chant /tʃɑ:nt/ verb: to sing.

charper /tʃɑ:pə/ verb: to seek. Parlyaree via Italian: *Cereare.*

charpering carsey /tʃɑpərɪŋ kɑ:si/ noun: a police station. Parlyaree.

charpering omee /tʃɑ:pərɪŋ əʊmi/ noun: a policeman. Parlyaree.

charver /tʃɑ:və/ verb: to fuck. Parlyaree.

charvering donna /tʃɑ:vərɪŋ dɒnə/ noun: a prostitute. Parlyaree.

chaud /ʃəʊd/ noun: penis.

chavvies /tʃævi:z/ noun: children. Parlyaree.

chemmie /tʃemi/ noun: a shirt or blouse. Probably from *chemise.*

cherry /tʃeri/ noun: a man's virginity.

chicken /'tʃɪkən/ 1. noun: an attractive man (usually aged under 25). 2. noun: a young boy.

chinker, chickwa /tʃɪnkə/ numeral: five. From Parlyaree via Italian: *cinque.*

cleaning the cage out /kli:nɪŋ ðə keɪdʒ aʊt/ verb: cunnilingus.

cleaning the kitchen /kli:nɪŋ ðə kɪtʃɪn/ verb: oral/anal sex (*rimming*).

clevie /klevi/ noun: vagina.

clobber /klɒbə/ noun: clothing.

cod /kɒd/ adjective: bad. Possibly derived from a usage of the word which originated in the fourteenth century, meaning scrotum (itself from the earlier definition of 'bag'), which is perhaps best known from the term *cod-piece.* However, from the seventeenth century onwards it become a slang word which could be applied to people, having a number of different forces including fool, honest man, old man (perhaps an abbreviation of *codger*), or drunken man. By the beginning of the twentieth century, *cod* was also slang for a joke, hoax or parody. One could speak of the 'cod' version of something, 'cod Victorian decorations' for example. The Polari meaning of *cod* is slightly different from this; having taken and distilled the negative connotations from *cod* meaning hoax, *cod* as Polari simply means something bad.

> Sandy: Right, right, well I'll just open the wardrobe. Oh, here, look – his wardrobe. Haaaa!
> Julian: Haaaaa! Oh what a naff lot!
> Sandy: It is a bit cod isn't it.
>
> Bona Rags

coddy, cody /kɒdi/ 1. adjective: bad, amateurish. Elaboration of *cod*. 2. noun: body. Truncation of **lucoddy**.

cods /kɒdz/ noun: testicles.

cold calling /kəʊld kɔ:lɪŋ/ verb: to walk into a pub looking for company.

colin /kɒlɪn/ noun: an erect penis.

coliseum curtains /kɒlə'si:əm kɜ:tɪnz/ noun: foreskin.

(the) colour of his eyes /kʌlə əv hɪz aɪz/ noun: penis size.

corybungus /kɒrɪbʌŋdʒəs/ noun: posterior.

cossy /kɒsi/ noun: *cossy* occurs once as a Polari word in *Round The Horne*. It is a truncation of *costume*, and appears to be fairly commonly known as the slang word *cozzy* or *cozzie* today, frequently heard in Australian soap operas and used to refer to 'swimming costume'. However, if it were not for Julian explicitly noting its Polari status, it would not have been included here:

Julian: Oh dear, I wonder if he's with BBC2? What cossy did they say?
Kenneth Horne: Cossy?
Julian: Costume. Polari for costume.
Kenneth Horne: Oh yes, they said a dinner-suit.
Bona Studios

cottage, cottaging /ˈkɒtɪdʒ/ noun: a public lavatory or urinal. *Cottage* first started being used to mean toilet at the beginning of the twentieth century. In British parks, the 'facilities' provided tended to look like miniature country cottages, with a sloping roof and windows, and homosexual men started to refer to them as such. Just as *camping* and *cruising* can be used as double entendres, so could phrases which involved *cottaging*: 'I'm just back from a lovely cottaging holiday in the Lake District'.

crimper /ˈkrɪmpə/ noun: a hairdresser.

crocus /krəʊkəs/ noun: a doctor. Possibly derived from the Latinized surname of Dr Helkiah Crooke, author of a *Description of the Body of Man* (1615).

cruise /ˈkru:z/ See **Main Entry**.

cull /kʌl/ noun: 1. mate. 2. fool. Cant, Molly slang. *Culls* are also used as a shortened version of *testicles*.

D

dacha, daiture, deger /deɪtʃə/ numeral: ten. From Parlyaree via Italian: *dieci*.

daffy /dæfi/ adjective: to be drunk on gin. Daffy's Elixir was a medicine given to infants, to which gin was often added.

dally /'dæli/ adjective: sweet, kind. Possibly an alternate pronunciation of **dolly**.

dash /'dæʃ/ verb: leave quickly.

deaner, deener, dener, diener /di:nə/ noun: a shilling.

dear /dɪə/ (also *dearie*) noun: used as a friendly yet rather patronizing personal term of address. To be called *dear* may imply that someone is unable to remember your name.

delph /delf/ noun: teeth.

dewey, dooe, dooey, duey /'dju:ɪ/ /du:ɪ/ numeral: two. Parlyaree via Italian: *due*.

dhobie, dohbie /'dəʊbi/ verb: to wash. noun: washing. From nautical slang, although the word originally comes from the Hindi *dhobi*: an Indian washerman.

diddle /'dɪdəl/ noun: gin. A *diddle-cove* was the keeper of a gin or spirit shop. In the US the word meant liquor.

(the) dilly /'dɪli/ noun: a shortened version of *Piccadilly Circus*: a part of central London that was a popular hang-out and pick-up place for Polari-speaking male prostitutes.

dilly boy /'dɪli bɔɪ/ noun: a male prostitute.

dinarly, dinarla, dinaly /dɪnɑ:li/ noun: money. Spanish: *dinero*. Italian: *denaro*.

dinge /dɪndʒ/ adjective: black. A *dinge queen* was a gay man who sought out black partners.

> 'When I saw you having a vada in the dinge section, I said to myself, Andrea – my name's Andy in real life actually, dear – Andrea, I said to myself, there's a gay one if ever I saw one.'
>
> Michael Carson (1988: 203) *Sucking Sherbert Lemons*

dish /dɪʃ/ noun: 1. an anus. 2. an attractive man. The original meaning was associated with food – terms to do with food are often used metaphorically to imply sex or attractiveness e.g. **chicken**, *beefcake*. A more recent gay (but not Polari) use of *dish* as a verb means to tell someone what you think of them.

dish the dirt /diʃ ðə dɜ:t/ verb: to talk things over, gossip.

dizzy /dɪzi/ adjective: scatterbrained.

do a turn /du: ə tɜ:n/ verb: have sex. Most likely derived from theatrical slang, but also used among homosexual men in the Merchant Navy.

do the rights /du: ðə raɪts/ verb: to seek revenge.

dog and bone /dɒg ən 'bəʊn/ noun: a telephone. From Cockney rhyming slang.

dolly /dɒli/ 1. noun: a smart or attractive woman. Can also be used as a term of address: 'It's ages since I've seen you, dolly!'

2. adjective: attractive (e.g. dolly-bird):

> Sandy: Oh yes we're filling in as photographers between acting engagements on the telly. We just done this

one where I'm all dragged up as a Sultan squatting on me cushion. All surrounded by these dolly little palones.

Studio Bona

3. Bruce Rodgers (1972: 65), in his American-based gay lexicon translates *dolly* as meaning penis, as well as attractive. However, it is not certain if this would have been known by the *Round the Horne* writers, who used the word in its adjectival sense.

Dolly most likely began as a pet-name for Dorothy, and as early as the seventeenth century was being used to refer to a drab, slattern or useless woman. By the early twentieth century, its meaning had changed to refer to a pleasant attractive woman. By the 1970s, *dolly* could be used on men as well as women – for example, a gay porn magazine of the 1970s was called *The Dolly Male*.

dona, donner, donah, doner /dɒnə/ noun: a woman. From Parlyaree probably via Italian.

don't be strange /dəʊnt biː streɪndʒ/ imperative: don't hold back.

dorcas /dɔːkəs/ noun: term of endearment, 'one who cares'. The Dorcas Society was a ladies' church association of the nineteenth century, which made clothes for the poor.

dowry /ˈdaʊri/ quantifier: a lot.

drag /dræg/ See **Main Entry**.

drag up /dræg ʌp/ verb: to wear woman's clothes.

drage /dreɪʒ/ noun: drag.

dress up /dres ʌp/ noun: a bad (as in unconvincing) drag queen.

drogle /drəʊgəl/ noun: a dress.

dubes, doobs, doobies /du:bz/ noun: 1. pills. 2. marijuana cigarettes.

duchess /ˈdʌtʃəs/ noun: a rich or grand gay man.

ducky, duckie /dʌki/ noun. Term of address, used in a similar way to **dear**. In the sixteenth century *ducky* was used to refer to a woman's breast, but by the nineteenth century it was used as a term of affection.

dyke, dike /deɪk/ noun: a lesbian. See **Main Entry**.

E

ear fakes /ɪə feɪkz/ noun: earrings.

ecaf /ˈi:kæf/ noun: a face. Derived from backslang (the backwards spelling of *face*).

eek, eke /i:k/ noun: a face. Truncated and more familiar form of **ecaf**, as this Polari version of the song 'Baby Face' shows:

> Bona eke, you've got the campest little bona eke
> And when you vada me if leaves me weak, bona eke
> My heart stops a racket every time I see your packet
> Nightclub Act, Lee Sutton

efink /i:fiŋk/ noun: a knife. From back-slang.

eine /aɪn/ noun: London.

emag /i:mæg/ noun: a game. From back-slang.

ends /endz/ noun: hair.

esong /ˈi:sɒŋ/ noun: a nose. Derived from back-slang.

F

fab /fæb/ adjective: great. Original truncation of *fabulous*.

fabe /feɪb/ adjective: great. Most likely an expansion on **fab**.

fabel /feɪbəl/ adjective: good. Possibly a blend of *fab* and *belle*.

fabulosa /fæbju:ˈləʊsə/ adjective: wonderful. A play on *fabulous*. The *-ulosa* ending links the word to Italian. Also from Spanish: *fabuloso*.

fag /fæg/ noun: a gay man. See **Main Entry**.

fag hag /fæg hæg/ noun: the female friend of a gay man.

fairy /feəri:/ noun: an effeminate homosexual man. See **Main Entry**.

fake /feɪk/ 1. noun: an erection. 2. verb: to make. 3. adjective: used as a stem to imply that something is false or artificially constructed in some way. From Italian: *faccio*.

fakement /feɪkmənt/ noun: 1. a thing. 2. personal adornment. Derived from *fake*.

fake riah /feɪk 'raɪə/ noun: a wig.

fambles /fæmbəlz/ noun: hands. Also *famble cheat*: ring; *fambler*: a glove. Sixteenth century slang. The original sense of the word most likely meant to grope or fumble.

fang carsey /fæŋ kɑ:zi/ noun: a dentist's surgery. Also *fang faker, fang crocus*: dentist. Fangs were teeth.

fantabulosa /fæntæbju:'ləʊsə/ adjective: wonderful. Most likely derived from *fantabulous*, a blend of *fabulous* and *fantastic*, occurring in the late 1950s. The *-ulosa* ending gives it the Italian/Polari sound.

farting crackers /fɑ:tɪŋ krækəz/ noun: trousers.

fashioned /fæʃənd/ adjective: synonym of the adjectival use of *fake*.

fashioned riah /fæʃənd 'raɪə/ noun: a wig.

fatcha /fætʃə/ verb: shave, apply make-up. From Italian: *faccia*.

feely, feele, feelier, fellia /fi:li/ noun: a young person or a child. From Italian: *figlie*.

femme /fem/ noun: 1. female. 2. a feminine lesbian. US slang.

ferricadooza /fɜ:i:kædu:zə/ noun: a knock-down blow. The stem *ferri-* refers to something made of iron, while *caduca* means 'fall' in Italian.

filiome /fi:liɪəʊmi/ noun: 1. a young man. 2. an underaged sexual partner. Derived from a combination of **feely** and **omee**. From Italian. See **feely**.

filly /fɪli/ adjective: pretty.

fish /fɪʃ/ noun: woman (derogatory).

flange /ˈflændʒ/ 1. noun: vagina. One of the original eighteenth century uses of *flange* refers to a projecting flat rim, collar or rib, used to strengthen an object, to guide it, to keep it in place or to facilitate its attachment to another object. 2. verb: to walk along.

flatties /flæti:z/ noun: men (especially those who make up an audience). The female equivalent is **gillies**. The term *flattie* is slightly derogatory, originally meaning one who is ignorant of the ways of professional thieving, and therefore a dupe.

flowery /ˈflaʊəri/ noun: lodgings, accommodation. A *flowery dell* is nineteenth century rhyming slang for prison cell.

fogle /ˈfəʊgəl/ noun: a handkerchief or neckerchief (usually silk). A *fogle-hunter* was a pickpocket.

fogus /fəʊgəs/ noun: tobacco. Seventeenth century slang, derived most likely from the word *fog*, which was used to mean smoke.

foofs /fu:fs/ noun: breasts.

fortuni /fɔ:tʃu:ni/ adjective: gorgeous.

frock /frɒk/ noun: female attire.

frock billong lallies /frɒk bɪlɒŋ læli:z/ noun: trousers. Adapted from Tok Pisin where the word *billong* means 'belonging to'.

fruit /fru:t/ noun: a gay man. Originally US or prison slang.

full drag /fʌl dræg/ noun: completely decked out in women's attire e.g. 'Betty's got the full drag on tonight!' See **drag**.

full eke /fʌl i:k/ noun: wearing make-up. See **eek**.

fungus /'fʌŋgəs/ noun: an old man.

funt /fʊnt/ noun: a pound.

G

gajo /gædʒəʊ/ noun: outsider. From Romany.

gam /gæm/ noun: 1. oral sex. Shortening of the French: *gamahuche*. 2. leg. Possibly coming from *gamb* or *gambe*, the northern form of *jambe* which means the 'leg of an animal represented on a coat of arms'.

gamming /gæmɪŋ/ verb: oral sex. From **gam**.

gamp /gæmp/ noun: umbrella. After Mrs Sarah Gamp, a nurse in Dickens' *Martin Chuzzlewit*, who carried a large cotton umbrella.

gardy loo /gɑ:di lu:/ vocative: look out! Originally used when the contents of a chamber pot were thrown out of a window. From pseudo-French *gare de l'eau* 'beware of the water' (the correct version would be *gare l'eau*).

gay /geɪ/ See **Main entry**.

gelt /gelt/ noun: money. Most likely from German.

gent /dʒent/ noun: money. Variant pronunciation of **gelt**, or perhaps from the French *argent*.

gildy /gɪldi/ adjective: fancy. Used in the film *Velvet Goldmine*. 'A tart in gildy clobber' – 'A slut in fancy clothes'.

gillies /dʒɪli:s/ noun: women (especially those in an audience). From Parlyaree.

girl /gɜ:l/ noun: term of address, similar in meaning to *ducky, dear, heartface* etc. These words are often used as a kind of full-stop at the end of every sentence: '. . . dolly ecafe, girl!'

glory hole /ˈglɔ:ri həʊl/ noun: hole between two stalls in a toilet or *cottage* – usually big enough to poke things through. Smaller holes which are only big enough to look through are generally referred to as *peep-holes*. It's likely that this word originated from navy or army slang. In the navy a *glory-hole* was any of the various compartments on a ship, or one or more rooms used as sleeping quarters for stewards (of whom a significant proportion were homosexual, at least in the merchant navy). In army slang, a *glory-hole* was an expression for any small billet or dug-out.

glossies /ˈglɒsi:z/ noun: magazines. US slang.

goolie /ˈgu:li/ adjective: black.

goolie ogle fakes /ˈgu:li əʊgəl feɪks/ noun: sunglasses.

got your number /gɒt jʊə nʌmbə/ verb phrase: if you've 'got someone's number' you know what they're up to, or you know they're homosexual. A favourite of Julian and Sandy:

> Kenneth Horne: Now if you're referring to Miss Fifi La Bootstrap.
> Julian: Yes we are.
> Kenneth Horne: She's a talented cabaret artiste.
> Sandy: Oooh!
> Kenneth Horne: Yes I was helping her with her career.
> Sandy: Oooh! Helping her, that's alright ducky, we've *all* got your number!
>
> Bona Tax Consultants

groin, groyne /grɔɪn/ noun: a ring.

groinage /groinədʒ/ noun: jewellery.

gutless /gʌtləs/ adjective: either very good or very bad.

H

hambag, handbag /ˈhæmbæg/ noun: money.

hampsteads /ˈhæmpstəds/ noun: teeth. Cockney rhyming slang via *Hampstead Heath*.

harris /hærəs/ noun: arse. Likely to be derived from **aris**.

head /hed/ noun: toilet.

hearing cheat /hi:rɪŋ tʃi:t/ noun: ear. Cant – literally a *hearing thing*.

heartface /'hɑ:t feɪs/ noun: term of address. Used in a similar way to *dear*. These terms of address can be used sarcastically or ironically – *heartface*, for example, when used on an old or unattractive man can be quite insulting.

> Julian: Now how can we help you, visage de couer?
> Sandy: That's French for heartface!
>
> Bona School of Languages

Hilda Handcuffs /hɪldə 'hænkʌfs/ noun: the police.

HP /eɪtʃ pi:/ noun: a gay man. Derived from the initial letters of *homee palone*.

husband /'hʌzbənd/ noun: a male lover, usually more than just a one-night stand, but can be used ironically to refer to any short-term sexual partner. See also **wedding night**.

I

importuning /ɪmpɔ:'tʃu:nɪŋ/ verb: street 'trading'. Ironic and often bitter use of legalese.

in the life /ɪn ðə laɪf/ adjective: euphemism for *homosexual*.

irish /aɪrɪʃ/ noun: a wig. From Cockney rhyming slang – Irish jig.

it /ɪt/ pronoun: used to refer to a short-term sexual partner.

J

jarry /dʒa:ri/ verb: to eat. Derived from the Parlyaree word *munjaree*. It is especially used to refer to eating something sexually: e.g. *jarry the cartes* (to fellate).

Jennifer Justice /dʒenəfə dʒʌstɪs/ noun: the police.

jew's eye /dʒu:z aɪ/ noun: anything of value. From sixteenth century slang.

jim and jack /dʒɪm ən dʒæk/ noun: a back. From rhyming slang.

jogger, jogar /dʒɒgə/ verb: 1. to play. 2. to sing. 3. to entertain. From Italian: *giocare* (play/game).

joggering omee /dʒɒgərɪŋ əʊmi/ noun: an entertainer.

joshed up /ʒu:ʃd ʌp/ adjective: looking your best. See **zhoosh**.

jubes, joobs /dʒu:bz/ noun: breasts (female). Also pectorals (male).

K

kaffies /kæfi:z/ noun: trousers.

kapello /kæ'peləʊ/ noun: a cloak. From Italian: *capello*.

ken /ken/ noun: a house. From Cant.

kenza /kenzə/ numeral: twelve.

kerterver cartzo /kɜ:tɜ:və kɑ:tzəʊ/ noun: a venereal disease. Literally *bad genitals*. *Kerterver* is a variant of **catever**.

kosher homie /kəʊʃə həʊmi/ noun: a Jewish man. From Hebrew.

L

lady /leɪdi/ noun: a homosexual male.

lag, lage /læg/ 1. noun: a convict or prisoner. 2. verb: to urinate.

lallie, lally, lall, lyle, /læli/ noun: a leg. Also *lally-pegs* (possible rhyming slang for *legs*).

lally-covers /læli kʌvəs/ noun: trousers.

lally-drags /læli drægz/ noun: trousers. Also *vally-drags*, although this may be a mis-spelling.

lamor /læ'mɔ:/ noun: a kiss. From French.

lappers /læpəz/ noun: hands.

large /lɑ:dʒ/ superlative. See **mental**.

lattie /'læti/ noun: a house or flat. From Parlyaree, where its original meaning referred to the lodgings used by itinerant actors.

lattie on water /'læti ɒn wɔ:tə/ noun: a ship. Literally a *house on water*.

lattie on wheels /'læti ɒn wi:lz/ noun: a car or taxi. Literally a *house on wheels.*

lau /laʊ/ verb: to place or to put. Used in the Julian and Sandy phrase *order lau your luppers on the strillers bona.*

lav /læv/ noun: a word. The phrase *bona lavs* can be used as a sign off to a letter meaning 'best wishes'.

lell /lel/ verb: to take.

lepta /leptə/ numeral: eleven.

letch water /letʃ wɔ:tə/ noun: pre-cum.

letties /'leti:z/ noun: lodgings. From Italian *letto: bed.*

letty /'leti/ 1. noun: a bed. 2. verb: to sleep. From Italian *letto: bed.*

libbage /lɪbɪdʒ/ noun: bed, or any sleeping quarters. Cant. *Lib* was sleep.

lills /lɪlz/ noun: hands.

lily, lilly /lɪli/ noun: the police. From *Lily Law.*

ling grappling /lɪŋ græplɪŋ/ noun: sex. Originally, to *ling* was to stick the tongue out of the mouth.

lingo /lɪŋgəʊ/ noun: foreign language.

lippy /'lɪpi/ noun: lipstick.

long dedger /lɒŋ dedʒə/ numeral: eleven.

lucoddy /lu:kɒdi/ noun: body. Cockney rhyming slang.

lullaby cheat /lʊləbai tʃi:t/ noun: a baby.

luppers /lʊpəz/ noun: fingers.

M

mais oui /meɪ wi:/ vocative: of course. French.

manky /mæŋki/ adjective: bad, poor, tasteless. From 1950s UK slang. Possibly influenced by the French *manqué*.

manly alice /mænli: ælɪs/ noun: a masculine gay man.

maquiage /ˈmæki:ɑ:ʒ/ noun: make-up. From French *maquiller*: to make up one's face.

maria /mæri:ə/ noun: sperm.

mart covers /mɑ:t kʌvəz/ noun: gloves.

martini /mɑ:ti:ni/ noun: a ring.

marts, martinis /mɑ:ts/ noun: hands. Possibly from French *main*. See also **sweet and dry**.

Mary, Mary-Ann /meəri/ noun: 1. a generic term for any gay man. 2. a Catholic gay man. 3. Exclamation. *Oh Mary!* Also *Muscle Mary* – one who spends too long in the gym. Likely origins, Mollie slang and/or US gay slang.

matlock mender /ˈmætlɒk mendə/ noun: a dentist.

matlocks /ˈmætlɒks/ noun: teeth.

mauve /məʊv/ adjective: someone who appears homosexual e.g. 'she's mauve!'.

mazarine /mæzəri:n/ noun: a platform below stage. Theatrical slang.

measures, medzers, metzers, metzes /meʒəz/ noun: money.

meat and two veg /mi:t ən tu: vedʒ/ noun: a man's penis and testicles. Euphemism.

meat rack /mi:t ræk/ noun: 1. a male brothel. 2. any place where large numbers of men are sexually available.

medzer caroon /medzə kə'ru:n/ noun: a half crown.

medzer, madzer /medzə/ noun: half. From Italian: *mezzo*.

mental /mentəl/ superlative: 'That's mental' – that's the best! (or the worst). 1960s slang.

meshigener /meʃɪgnə/ adjective: crazy. From Yiddish.

metties, metzies /meti:z/ noun: money. From the word *metal*.

mezsh /meʒ/ noun: money. Contraction of *measures*.

mince /mɪns/ verb: to walk with short steps in an affected manner. *Mince* dates back to the sixteenth century, and was originally used to describe the movement of females. By the middle of the eighteenth century, the verb was used with reference to males ('The men are all puppies, mincing and dancing and chattering', Foote, 1753).

Julian: Through these portals have minced England's top male models.

Bona Male Models

minces /mɪnsəz/ noun: eyes. Derived from Cockney Rhyming Slang. *Mince pies* are eyes.

minge /mɪndʒ/ noun: a vagina. Derogatory. Early twentieth century slang, most likely from the army or navy and used to refer to female company. Linked with *binge* (alcohol) e.g. 'His problem is minge, mine is binge.'

minnie /mɪni/ 1. noun: a homosexual man. 2. verb: to walk.

moey, mooe /ˈmu:i/ noun: 1. a mouth. 2. a face. From Romany *mooi.*

mogue /məʊg/ verb: to mislead or lie.

molly /mɒli/ noun: a homosexual man. Also *margery.*

montrel /mɒntrel/ noun: a clock or watch. From French *montre.*

mother /mʌðə/ pronoun: me, myself. Often used by older gay men to friends when they're talking about themselves, especially in the phrase *your mother*: 'pull up a chair and tell your mother all about it'.

muck /mʌk/ noun: stage make-up. From theatrical slang.

mudge /mʌdʒ/ noun: a hat.

multy, multi, mutlee /mʌlti/ quantifier: very, much, many, a lot. From Italian: *molto.*

May all our dolly Sisters & Brothers in the order receive multee orgasmic visitations from the spirit of Queer Power in 1998.

Blessing from the London Order of The Sisters of Perpetual Indulgence

mungaree, mangare, munjarry, manjarie, manjaree, monjaree, munja, numgare /mən'dʒɒ:ri/ 1. noun: food. 2. verb: to eat. *Mungaree* probably comes from Parlyaree via the Italian *mangiare* (to eat). See also **jarry**.

munge /mʌndʒ/ noun: darkness.

N

nada /nɑ:də/ quantifier: none. The term *nada to vada in the larder* means that someone is not particularly well endowed.

naff, naph /'næf/ adjective: 1. tasteless. 2. heterosexual.

Naff is a word which has found its way into late twentieth century English slang and is used among heterosexuals and homosexuals alike. However, it has an intriguing history as a Polari word. The *Oxford English Dictionary* (1994) cites the word *niffy-naffy* as meaning inconsequential or stupid. One story claims that it began as an acronym slang-word used by the American army in World War II, meaning *Not Available For Fucking*, but somehow passed over into the gay male lexicon at this time. This is credible – in *The Naked Civil Servant* Quentin Crisp describes how once the Americans entered the war, London became full of sexually available uniformed men.

Partridge (1970), however claims that *naff* is prostitutes' slang, and gives two possibilities as to its origins: one from the French *rien a faire*, the other from *not a fuck*. As well as the original acronym, Hugo Young suggests that *naff* could stand for *Normal as Fuck*, or as a truncation of the slang phrase *Nawfuckingood*. Another slang Forces acronym in Partridge's slang dictionary is *Naffy (N.A.A.F.I.)* which means *No aim, ambition or fucking initiative*, also *No Ambition an Fuck-all Interest* (from email correspondence with Paul Larkhall), so perhaps *naff* is a truncation derived from *Naffy*. James Gardiner (1997) cites *naf* in his Polari lexicon as being back-slang from *fanny*.

Another source claims the word originated in the late 1970s after the arrival of the National Association for Freedom (NAF) 'Naff off!' was a term hurled by CPBM-L (Communist Party of Great Britain Marxist-Leninist) students at their extreme right-wing fellow students (from email correspondence with Isabel H, Vancouver). However, as Julian and Sandy were already using *naff* as a Polari word in the late 1960s, we can probably discount this.

Given that nine possible origins of the word *naff* are listed here, it is unlikely that any one source can be held responsible for its creation. Nor is it possible to determine which source (if any) came first. However, either by the army, prostitutes or French, it found its way into the Polari lexicon. Once taken up by gay men, it was used as a Polari word to refer to objects, people, items of clothing etc. which were of bad taste, ugly or not worth bothering about sexually because they were heterosexual:

Sandy: Oh those horrible little naff gnomes. Oh no!

Bona Homes

Sandy: You've got to sell yourself. Go on.
Julian: No. In a close-up my knees is dead naff. I mean they're all wrinkled.

Bona Promotions

By the 1980s, *naff* had crossed over into mainstream English slang, meaning something worthless or tasteless: 'It is naff to call your house The Gables, Mon Repos or Dunroamin' *Sunday Telegraph*, 21st August 1983. Although it came to be used by heterosexuals, the original meaning of *naff* – as a pejorative word levelled at them by gay men was not widely known. The new users would have understood the semantics of the word, but not the initial target. By this time, however, the 'ownership' and the target of the word had changed sufficiently for the original meaning not to matter.

namyarie, nanyarie /'næmjɑ:ri/ 1. verb: to eat. 2. noun: food. A possible variant of **mungaree**.

nanna /nɑ:nə/ adjective: awful.

nanti, nantee, nanty, nunty, nuntee /nænti/ negator: can be used to mean *no, none, don't* or *nothing*:

> Kenneth Horne: I'm suffering from insomnia.
> Julian: Nanti kip eh?
>
> Bona Nature Clinic

> Normally my sister is a regular Miss Mouse. Not for nothing is she called The N. P. P., the nanty-polare-palone.
>
> James Gardiner (1997) *Who's A Pretty Boy Then?*

From Italian: *niente*.

nanti dinarly /nænti dɪnɑ:li/ noun phrase: no money.

nanti polari, nanty panarly /nænti pæ'lɑ:ri/ imperative: don't say anything.

nanti pots in the cupboard /nænti pɒtz ɪn ðə kʌpbəd/ no teeth.

nanti that /nænti ðæt/ imperative: leave it alone, forget about it.

nantoise, nantoisale /næntwɑ:/ 1. negator: no. 2. adjective: inadequate.

nanty worster /nænti wɜ:stə/ vocative: no worse.

nawks /ˈnɔ:ks/ noun: bosom.

nelly /ˈneli/ noun: an effeminate gay man.

nellyarda /neli:ɑ:də/ verb: to listen.

nishta, nish, nishtoise, nishtoisale /nɪʃtə/ negator: nothing, no. Similar to **nix**.

nix /nɪks/ negator: don't, no, not. Possibly from German *nichts*. *Nix my dolly* meant *never mind*. To *keep nix* was to keep watch in nineteenth century slang.

nix mungarlee /nɪks mʊndʒɑ:li/ noun-phrase: nothing to eat.

nobber /nɒbə/ 1. numeral: nine. 2. noun: one who collects money for a street performer. From Italian: *nove*.

nochy /nɒtʃi/ noun: night. From Italian: *notte*. Spanish: *noche*.

nosh /nɒʃ/ noun, verb: to perform oral sex. From Yiddish.

NTBH /en ti: bi: aɪtʃ/ adjective: not available, or ugly. Acronym of *Not To Be Had*.

number /ˈnʌmbə/ noun: a person, usually sexually attractive: 'check out the butch number over there!'.

O

ogale fakes /əʊgəl feɪks/ noun: spectacles. This compound noun is sometimes used with the order of its component parts reversed: *fake ogales*.

ogle /ɒgəl/ /əʊgəl/ 1. verb: to look longingly at a man. 2. noun: eyes. From eighteenth century Cant. Also Italian: *occhio* (eye).

ogle filters /ɒgəl fɪltəz/ noun: sunglasses (see also **ogle shades**).

ogle riahs /ɒgəl raɪəz/ noun: eyelashes.

ogle riah fakes /ɒgəl raɪə feɪks/ noun: false eye lashes.

ogle riders /ɒgəl raɪdəz/ noun: eyebrows or eyelashes. Most likely derived because they 'ride' above the eyes, or as a possible mishearing of **ogle riahs**.

ogle shades /ɒgəl ʃeɪdz/ noun: sunglasses/glasses.

omee, omi, omy, omme, omer, homee, homi /ˈəʊmi/ noun: a man. *Omee* has a long history, coming to Polari as a Parlyaree word used by actors to refer to each other. It is most likely a corruption of the Italian word for man: *uomo*. *Omee* is first recorded in Hotton's Dictionary of Slang (1864), meaning master or landlord. By the end of the nineteenth century it had come to have a more general meaning as man. The additional /h/ sound at the beginning of the word was probably added as a result of contact with East London communities, which co-incidentally takes it close to the word *homo*. However, for most Polari speakers the /h/ is usually silent.

omee-palone, homee-palone /ˈəʊmi pəˈləʊn/ noun: a homosexual man. The word is a combination of **omee** (man) and **palone** (woman), meaning man-woman.

> Sandy: We can get you the great omee-palone. He's one of ours, isn't he Jules?
>
> Bona Performers

oney /wɒni/ numeral: one.

onk /ɒnk/ noun: a nose.

on the team /ɒn ðə tiːm/ adjective: gay.

on your tod /ɒn jɔː tɒd/ adjective: alone. Rhyming slang. Short for *Tod Sloan* (occasionally used in full) the name of a US jockey (1874–1933).

opals, ocals /ˈəʊpəlz/ noun: eyes.

orbs /ɔːbz/ noun: eyes.

order, orderly /ˈɔːdəli/ verb: 1. to leave, to go. 2. to experience orgasm (e.g. to come). From Parlyaree.

orderly daughters /ɔːdəli dɔːtəz/ noun: the police.

otter /ɒtə/ numeral: eight. From Italian: *octo*.

outrageous /aʊtˈreɪdʒəs/ adjective: extrovert, loud, camp.

oyster /ˈɔɪstə/ noun: a mouth.

P

packet /pækɪt/ noun: a man's crotch. Also *lunch, bulge.*

palaver /pəlɑ:və/ 1. verb: to talk. 2. noun: an argument. From Italian: *palare* (to talk).

palliass /pæli:æs/ noun: a back.

palone, polone, polony, pollone, paloney, polonee, palogne /pə'ləʊn/ noun: a woman, girl. *Palone* possibly comes from the seventeenth century slang word *blowen* meaning wench or prostitute. It can also be used to mean an effeminate man.

palone-omee /pə'ləʊn 'əʊmi/ noun: a lesbian. Just as **omee-palone** means homosexual man, the reverse ordering means lesbian.

pannam, pannum /pænəm/ noun: bread.

parker /'pɑ:kə/ verb: 1. to pay out. 2. to give. From Italian: *pagare* (to pay).

parkering ninty /pɑ:kərɪŋ nɪnti/ noun: wages.

parker the measures /'pɑ:kə ðə meʒʌz/ verb: to pay the money.

parnie, parnee, parney /'pɑ:ni/ noun: 1. rain water. 2. tears.

passive /pæsɪv/ adjective: a homosexual man who takes the insertee role in anal intercourse and may also be quiet and effeminate.

pastry cutter /'peɪstri kʌtə/ noun: a man whose oral sex technique involves digging into the skin of the penis with his teeth.

pearls /pɜ:lz/ noun: teeth.

phantom /fæntəm/ noun: from *phantom gobbler*. A phantom would usually be a closeted gay man in the Merchant Navy who would go round the cabins at night, lifting the sheets of the other sailors to administer oral sex while they slept (or pretended to sleep). See also **BMQ**.

pig /pɪg/ noun: an elephant.

pig's lattie /pɪgz læti/ noun: a sty on the eye. One of the more creative uses of Polari: *pig's lattie* literally translates to 'pig's house', commonly known as a pigsty.

plate /pleɪt/ verb: to perform oral sex. Rhyming slang (and prostitute's slang) from *plate of ham* = **gam** which is a truncation of *gamahouche*. Also *plate* is rhyming slang for *fellate* or *plates of meat* = *eat*. To *plate someone's dish* is to **rim** them.

plates /pleɪts/ noun: feet. Cockney rhyming slang from *plates of meat*.

pogy, pogey /pəʊgi:/ adverb: a little. From Italian: *poco*.

polari, polare, palare, parlaree /pæ'lɑ:ri/ 1. noun: gay language. 2. verb: to talk. Most likely from Italian: *palare*.

polari lobes /pæ'lɑ:ri ləʊbs/ noun: ears.

polari pipe /pæ'lɑ:ri paɪp/ noun: a telephone.

poll /pɒl/ noun: a wig. Molly slang.

pont, ponce /pɒnt/ noun: a pimp. From French: *pont*.

ponte, poona /pɒnt/ noun: a pound (monetary unit). From Italian: *pondo* (weight).

pots /'pɒtz/ noun: teeth.

pouf /pu:f/ noun: a homosexual man.

pretty face /prɪti feɪs/ noun: an attractive man.

punk /pʌnk/ noun: a male homosexual.

purple hearts /pɜ:pəl 'hɑ:ts/ noun: the drug Drinamyl.

putting on the dish /pʌtɪŋ ɒn ðə dɪʃ/ verb: to apply KY jelly to the anus, in preparation for anal sex. Also *putting on the brandy*.

Q

quarter, quater /kwɔ:tə/ numeral: four. From Italian: *quattro*.

quartereen /kwɔ:təri:n/ noun: a farthing.

quean's dolly /kwi:nz dɒli/ noun: a female friend of a gay man.

queen, quean /kwi:n/ noun: *queen* is a slang word used by many Polari speakers to refer to themselves, although like *trade*, it is a word which holds several meanings, which are dependant on the user, the target and the context of the situation. *Queen* was a word which the Mollies used on one another, although as a slang word, it has a history of being used on women, as much, or more than men. A female who was known as a queen, was either one whose rank or pre-eminence (often in a specified sphere) was comparable to that of a queen (Beauty Queen, Queen of Hearts, May Queen), an attractive girl, a girl-friend, or in parts of the country (e.g. Lancashire), a slang term of address similar to that of **dear**. The homosexual use of *queen*, is probably taken from an older word *quean*, which from the Middle Ages meant a woman, especially one who was ill-behaved, a jade, a hussy, a harlot or strumpet. Both *queen* and *quean* resulted from the rejoining of two related Old English words, *cwen* and *cwene*, rooted in the common Indo-European based *gwen* (meaning woman). One form became used to denote those at the top of the social scale (royalty, those who were best at something etc.) while the other experienced downward mobility, and was eventually connected to homosexuality.

Queen can be used to refer to any gay man, but it can also refer to various types of gay men: those who are effeminate, those who take the **passive** role in intercourse, or older men. Used in conjunction with other nouns, *queen* can simply denote someone who is 'into' a particular sexual scene; for example, *drag queen* (a man who wears feminine clothing, not a transsexual), *seafood queen* (one who pursues sailors), *bean queen* (one who prefers Mexican partners) etc. Although *queen* may be aimed at homosexual men by outsiders with pejorative intent, used by homosexual men to each other, it is neutral or affectionate.

queeny /kwi:ni/ adjective: effeminate.

queer ken /kwi:ə ken/ noun: a prison. From Cant.

quongs /kwɒŋz/ noun: testicles.

R

randy comedown /rændi kʌmdaʊn/ noun: the desire to have sex after the effect of taking drugs starts to wear off. From 1960s drug-users slang.

rattling cove /rætəlɪŋ kəʊv/ noun: a taxi.

real /ri:əl/ adjective: really, i.e. not drag. *Real girl* is used to refer to someone who's not a **girl** (i.e. gay man) or a *drag queen* in the Polari sense.

reef /ri:f/ verb: to feel, especially to feel the genitals of a person. Initially *reef* was a criminal word meaning to pull up the lining of a pocket so as to steal the contents. Possibly derived from back-slang.

remould /ri:məʊld/ noun: sex-change.

rent /rent/ noun: male prostitute. Used as early as 1828 to refer to money or cash exchanged for 'criminal activity', *rent* had entered the slang lexicon used by the armed forces by the twentieth century. By the 1960s its slang meaning had narrowed to mean gay prostitution, and could now be used to refer to the prostitute rather than the fee.

renter /rentə/ noun: male prostitute.

riah /ˈraɪə/ noun: hair. Originates from back-slang – the word is simply *hair* spelt backwards.

riah shusher /ˈraɪə ʃʌʃə/ noun: a hairdresser. Literally, one who *shushes* or **zhooshes** the riah.

rim /rɪm/ verb: oral-anal sex. Early twentieth century US slang. Perhaps a variant of the verb *ream* – to stretch or reach.

rogering cheat /rɒdʒərɪŋ tʃi:t/ noun: a penis. Literally 'thing that fucks'. From Cant.

rosie /rəʊzi/ noun: rubbish bin. From nautical slang.

rough /rʌf/ noun: masculine aggressive man. As described by Quentin Crisp in *The Naked Civil Servant* (1968).

royal /rɔɪəl/ adjective: queenly.

S

sa, say /seɪ/ numeral: six. From Italian: *Sei.*

salter, saltee, salty, saulty /'sɒltə/ noun: a penny. From Italian *soldi.*

savvy /'sævi/ 1. verb: to know or to understand. *Savvy?* means *do you understand?* 2. noun: knowledge, practical sense, intelligence. Possibly from Jamaican-English via French or Spanish.

say dooe /seɪ du:i/ numeral: eight. Literally *six and two.* Most likely from Parlyaree.

say oney /seɪ wɒni/ numeral: seven. Literally *six and one.* Most likely from Parlyaree.

say tray /seɪ treɪ/ numeral: nine. Literally *six and three.* Most likely form Parlyaree

scarper, scaper, scarpy, scapali /'skɑ:pə/ verb: to run, to escape. Either from Italian *scappare,* or by rhyming slang: *scapa flow* – to go.

scat /skæt/ See **Main Entry**.

schinwhars, chinois /ʃinwɑ:z/ noun: a Chinese man or woman. From French.

schonk /ʃɒŋk/ verb: to hit. Possibly from Yiddish.

schumph /ʃʌmf/ verb: to drink. Possibly from Yiddish.

schvartza /'!vɑ:tsə/ noun: a black man. From Yiddish. Derogatory. Also *schvartza homie*: black man, *schvartza palone*: black woman.

scotches /'skɒtʃəz/ noun: legs. Rhyming slang from *scotch pegs.*

screaming /skri:mɪŋ/ adjective: loud effeminate mannerisms. Also *screaming queen:* outrageous gay man.

screech /skri:tʃ/ noun: 1. mouth. 'Oh, shut your screech'. 2. face.

screeve /skri:v/ 1. verb: to write. 2. noun: written material. Parlyaree.

seafood /si:fu:d/ noun: a (homo)sexually available sailor.

sea queen /si: kwi:n/ noun: 1. a gay sailor, particularly a steward or waiter in the Merchant Navy. 2. a gay man with a particular penchant for having sex with sailors.

send up /send ʌp/ verb: to make fun of.

setter /setə/ numeral: seven.

shamshes /ʃæmʃəz/ noun: possible back-slang for *smashers*. From Kenneth William's diary (Davies, 1994), Friday 24 October 1947 'Met 2 marines – very charming. Bonar Shamshes.'

sharda /'ʃɑ:də/ vocative: what a pity. From German, introduced into a version of Polari used in Ipswich in the 1970s.

sharper, sharp /ʃɑ:pə/ 1. verb: to steal. 2. noun: a policeman. Parlyaree, most likely a variant spelling of *charper*.

sharping-omee /ʃɑ:pɪŋ 'əʊmi/ noun: a policeman.

she /ʃi:/ pronoun: third person. 1. used on women. 2. or to refer to gay men: '*She*'s a wicked queen!'. 3. or to refer to heterosexual men, sometimes in order to deliberately undermine a case of self-assured masculinity. Also *her*.

sheesh /ʃi:ʃ/ adjective: showy, fussy, elaborately ornamented or unnecessarily affected, *sheesh* is probably a truncation of the French *chichi* (pronounced /ʃi:ʃi:/). Like **bijou**, it is another way of marking an object or thing as being connected in some way to homosexuality.

> Julian: Let's look through the wardrobe and see if we can find you some bona drag.
> Sandy: Here, here what about this? What about this? Very sheesh.
>
> BBC Studios

shush /ʃʌʃ/ verb: to steal. Possibly a variant of **zhoosh**.

shush bag /ʃʌʃ bæg/ noun: a swag bag.

shyckle, shyker, shietel /'ʃaɪkəl/ noun: a wig. From Yiddish *sheytl* – a wig worn by married women.

sister /sɪstə/ noun: a close friend, also likely to have once been an occasional sexual partner.

size queen /'saɪz kwi:n/ noun: one who likes well-endowed men.

slang /slæŋ/ verb: to perform on stage. Parlyaree.

slap /slæp/ noun: makeup.

sling-backs /slɪŋ bæks/ noun: high heels.

smellies /'smeli:z/ noun: perfume.

so /səʊ/ adjective: homosexual. 'Is he *so*?'

soldi /sɒldi/ noun: a penny. From Italian: *Soldi* (money).

solicit /sɒlɪsət/ verb: to **troll** while wearing **drag**. Borrowed legalese.

stamper /'stæmpə/ noun: a shoe. From Cant.

starters /stɑ:təz/ noun: any lubricant used for anal sex.

steamer /sti:mə/ noun: 1. the client of a prostitute. 2. gay man who seeks passive partners. From rhyming slang: steam tug = mug.

stiff /stɪf/ noun: paper. *Stiff* used to be slang for a forged note or cheque.

stimp covers /stɪmp kʌvəz/ noun: nylon stockings.

stimps /stɪmpz/ noun: legs.

stretcher-case /stretʃə keɪs/ adjective: exhausted. 'Your mother's a stretcher case.'

strides /straɪdz/ noun: trousers.

strillers /strɪləz/, **strills** /strɪlz/ noun: 1. a musical instrument. 2. a musician. Taken from Parlyaree and possibly the Italian word *strillare*.

strillers omee /strɪləz 'əʊmi/ noun: a pianist.

sweat chovey /swet tʃəʊvi/ noun: a gym or weights room.

sweet /swi:t/ adjective: good.

sweet and dry /swi:t ən draɪ/ noun: left and right. Used in conjunction with **martini**. A *sweet martini* was the right hand, while a *dry martini* was the left hand.

swishing /swɪʃɪŋ/ adjective: 1. acting flamboyantly grand. 2. acting effeminately camp.

T

tat /tæt/ adjective: rubbish. Tat has an early (seventeenth century) definition as loaded dice. In the nineteenth century it began to be associated with rags, poorly made or tasteless clothes and thus shabby people. Tat gatherers dealt in old rags. By the mid-twentieth century, *tat* had come to mean rubbish, junk or worthless goods. In twentieth century Australia the term is applied to false teeth.

Sandy: Mm, we may have a home for it. For instance, that bundle of rags, it may seem a useless load of old tat, but we'll take it off you.
Kenneth Horne: But that's the suit I'm wearing.
Bona Rags

TBH /ti: bi: aɪtʃ/ adjective: 1: sexually available. 2: gay. Acronym for *To Be Had*. See also **NTBH**. Popular from at least the 1920s, as described by Michael Davidson in *The World, The Flesh and Myself* (1962):

> The word 'queer', then hadn't been invented; the cryptic designation was 'so', corresponding *comme ça* in Montparnasse. 'Oh, is he *so*?' one would ask, giving a slight italic tone to the syllable. Another verbal cipher in use was the intials *t.b.h.* 'My dear,' someone might say standing outside Wellington Barracks, 'the one third from the right in the front rank – I know he's t.b.h!' – meaning 'to be had'; as the modern queer will say 'he's trade'.

that's your actual french /ðæts jə ækʃəl frentʃ/ idiom frequently used by Sandy in the Julian and Sandy sketches to highlight the use of (usually badly pronounced or pidgin) French, giving them a (mostly imagined) air of sophistication.

thews /θju:z/ noun: muscles, probably thighs but possibly used to refer to forearms. The *Oxford English Dictionary* (1994) gives one definition as being 'the bodily powers or forces of man ... muscle development associated with sinews, and hence materialised as muscles or tendons'.

Kenneth Horne: Could you give me some idea of his act?
Sandy: Well he comes on wearing this leopard skin you

see. He's a great butch omee, he's got these thews like an oak, and bulging lallies. Ohh!

Bona Performers

Thewes is used in several of Shakespeare's plays including Henry VI and Hamlet.

three drags and a spit /ðri: drægz ənd ə spit/ noun: a cigarette. The phrase *spit and drag* is rhyming slang for *fag*.

timepiece /'taɪm pi:s/ noun: a watch.

tip /tɪp/ verb: to perform oral sex.

tip the brandy /tɪp ðə brændi/ verb: to **rim**. Also *tongue the brandy*.

tip the ivy /tɪp ðə aɪvi/ verb: to **rim**.

tip the velvet /tɪp ðə velvət/ verb: 1. to perform oral sex. 2. to **rim**.

tittivate /tɪti:veɪt/ verb: to make oneself look pretty. Perhaps derived from the word *tidy*.

tober omee /təʊbə 'əʊmi/ noun: 1. a rent collector. 2. landlord. From Parlyaree.

tober showmen /təʊbə 'ʃəʊmən/ noun: travelling musicians. From Parlyaree. A *tober* is the site occupied by a circus, fair or market.

todge omee-palone /tɒdʒ 'əʊmɪ pə'ləʊn/ noun: the passive partner in gay sex.

toff omee /tɒf əʊmi/ noun: a rich older male partner or sugar daddy. *Toff* is perhaps a subversion of *tuft*, slang for a titled undergraduate (particularly at Oxford). A *tuft* was the ornamental gold tassle on a cap.

too much /tu: mʌtʃ/ adjective: excessive, over the top.

tootsie trade /ˈtʌtsi treɪd/ noun: the sexual pairing of two effeminate gay men.

tosheroon /tɒʃəru:n/ noun: half a crown.

town hall drapes /taʊn hɔ:l dreɪps/ noun: an uncircumcized penis.

trade /treɪd/ See **Main Entry**.

trade curtain /treɪd kɜ:tən/ noun: from Merchant Navy slang. Sailors sometimes were eight to a berth and in order to maintain a degree of privacy during homosexual sex, they would hang a curtain round their bunk.

tray /treɪ/ numeral: three.

treash /ˈtreʒ/ noun: term of endearment from Julian and Sandy. A truncation of *treasure.*

troll /trəʊl/ verb: *troll,* which has several meanings, is probably derived from an earlier definition which is to do with 'to move, walk about to and fro, ramble, saunter, stroll or roll', which dates back at least to the fourteenth century. Other definitions of *troll* are also to do with movement: it can be a bowling term, or mean 'to spin', 'to wag the tongue', 'to turn over in one's mind', 'to sing something in a round', or 'to draw on a moving bait'. Another meaning of *troll* is concerned with witchcraft; trolls were mythical creatures, formerly in Scandanavian mythology they were conceived as giants, and more recently as dwarves or imps. The word *trolla* in Sweden means 'to charm or bewitch'. It is possible that the Polari use of *troll* has taken aspects of both of these other sets of meanings into consideration: to walk around, seeking to charm a man into the act of copulation.

trollies /trəʊli:z/ noun: trousers. Derived perhaps from a combination of **lallies** and **troll**. A *trolley-dolly* (contemporary gay slang) is a gay flight attendant.

trummus /trʌməs/ noun: bum.

trundling cheat /trundəlɪŋ tʃi:t/ noun: a car.

turn my oyster up /tɜ:n maɪ ɔɪstə ʌp/ verb: to make me smile.

tush /tʌʃ/ noun: bum.

two and eight /tu: ənd eɪt/ noun: a state. 'Jim's in a right old two and eight'. From Cockney rhyming slang.

U

una /u:nə/ numeral: one. Parlyaree.

uppers and downers /ʌpəz ən daʊnəz/ noun: drugs.

V

vacaya /vækɑ:jə/ noun: originally used to refer to any mechanical or electrical device that emits sound, such as a jukebox or record player (e.g. 'cod sounds in the vacaya'), but has evolved to refer to mobile phones.

vada, varda, vardo, vardy, varder /ˈvɑːdə/ verb: to look. A *vardo* was a gypsy caravan in Romany, while in Lingua Franca the word meant to keep watch, or a warden.

vadavision, vardavision /ˈvɑːdəvɪʒən/ noun: a television.

vaf /væf/ imperative: acronym standing for 'Vada, absolutely fantabulosa!' upon seeing an attractive person.

vaggerie, vagary, vagarie /ˈveɪgəri/ verb: to go, to travel, to leave. Probably from Italian *vagare*.

vera /viːrə/ noun: gin. From rhyming slang: Vera Lynn = gin.

versatile /vɜːsətaɪl/ adjective: bisexual.

voche /vɒtʃi/ noun: 1. a voice. 2. a singer. From Italian: *voce*.

vodkatini /vɒdkətiːni/ noun: an alcoholic drink – a mixture of vodka and martini.

vogue /vəʊg/ 1. noun: a cigarette. 2. verb: to light (a cigarette). E.g. 'vogue us up ducky' from *A Storm in a Teacup*, (Channel 4, 1993).

vonka /ˈvɒnkə/ noun: a nose. Possibly Yiddish.

W

wallop /ˈwɒləp/ verb: to dance. Earlier meanings of this word included, to gallop, noisy bubbling movements made by water, a resounding blow or whack (which is the accepted usage today), an alcoholic drink, a flapping or fluttering rag, and a violent, clumsy, noisy movement of the body – suggesting that at one point to call a dancer a **walloper** might have implied that he or she wasn't very graceful. From Italian: *gallopare* (to dance on stage).

walloper /ˈwɒləpə/ noun: a dancer.

wedding night /ˈwedɪŋ naɪt/ noun: refers to the first time two men have sex together.

willets /wɪləts/ noun: breasts.

winkle /wɪŋkəl/ noun: a small penis. Initially the penis of a young boy.

Y

yews /ju:z/ noun: eyes.

your actual /jə ækʃəl/ an idiomatic phrase used by Julian and Sandy to emphasize something, e.g. 'that's your actual French', 'we are your actual homeopathic practioners'.

Z

zelda /zeldə/ noun: 1. a woman. 2. a witch.

zhoosh, jhoosh /ʒu:ʃ/ 1. noun: clothing:

> Julian: Oh come on, let's have a vada at his zhoosh.
> Kenneth Horne: Clothing, that's translator's note.
> Bona Rags

2. noun: trim or ornamentation. 3. verb: to zhoosh one's riah: to comb one's hair.

> Vada well, zhooshed riah, the shyckle mauve, full slap, rouge for days, fake ogle-riahs, fortuni cocktail frock and mother's fabest slingbacks.
>
> *A Storm in a Tea-cup*, Channel 4, 1993.

4. verb: to zhoosh off: to go away. 5. verb: to zhoosh something: to swallow something. 6. verb: to zhoosh oneself up: to titivate clothing or make-up.

One set of meanings of the word *zhoosh*, is derived from its onomatopoeic quality, and is concerned with a slipping or sliding movement: going away, taking things from a shop, or the action of something going down someone's windpipe. Another set has to do with personal appearance: clothing, doing one's hair, or titivating oneself.

zhooshy /ʒuːʃiː/ adjective: showy.

INTRODUCTION TO THE DICTIONARY OF GAY SLANG

Research into gay slang stretches back over a good deal of the twentieth century. One of the earliest gay lexicons was Gershon Legman's *The Language of Homosexuality: An American Glossary* (1941). This was a dictionary of homosexual male slang only – as apparently there were no terms used by lesbians because of their practice of 'gentlemanly restraint' – an association of lesbian speech with upper-class masculinity, whereas, conversely, gay speech was associated with lower-class femininity.

In 1965, Donald Cory published an article in *Sexology* called 'The Language of the Homosexual'. Cory describes two uses of homosexual slang: pejorative slang used by unfriendly heterosexuals, and secret 'insider' slang used by gay men in order to affirm membership and protect and strengthen the 'despised in-group'. Cory notes that often such words are stinging in their critical content, reflecting the two-sided feelings of gay people towards themselves. The article ends with a 40-word lexicon.

However, the largest and most well-known slang dictionary is *The Queen's Vernacular* published in 1972 by Bruce Rodgers. The ethos behind the book was to produce a dictionary of 'homosexual cant' – as the data was derived from participant observation the author had a claim to authenticity which he argued was lacking in most other gay glossaries. Consisting of several thousand entries the book is impressively large and is a result of 'years of interviews with hundreds of informants whom Rodgers sought out in bars, steam baths, dance halls, public johns and on street corners', implying that this is a work which charts spoken, rather than written language.

In 1972 the concept of Gay Liberation was still young.

In the thirty-odd years since then, gay men and lesbians have witnessed numerous social changes that would have been difficult to predict. The sense of hope inspired by the Gay Liberation movements of the early 1970s gave way to increased stigmatization of homosexuality as the 1980s progressed – gay communities were some of the first to feel the decimating effects of AIDS, and homophobic *schadenfreude* from some quarters. In the UK, Section 28 banned the promotion of homosexuality via local education authorities, in many cases preventing the subject from being discussed at all in schools. Debates over issues such as the age of consent, gay men and lesbians in the military and legal recognition of same-sex partnerships provoked controversy throughout the 1990s.

However, as gay men and lesbians gradually became more visible in the media, they began to be portrayed in more complex and interesting ways. Sexuality also became a commercial venture – the almost mythical 'pink pound' providing entrepreneurial opportunities, and encouraging the rise of numerous Gay Villages in Western cities. In the 1990s stigmatized and minority groups were united behind the concept of *Queer Theory* – anything that stood against the norm could be cast as queer – the meaning of the word being expanded to include not only *gay* but *lesbian, bisexual, transgendered, working class, black, S/M, Latino, disabled* and any other disenfranchised group. Queer theory was a return to in-your-face political action, reclaiming camp as a means of protest, and this dictionary takes a queer approach to gay and lesbian language by acknowledging the importance of words concerning groups such as transvestites, drag queens, transsexuals, bisexuals and BDSM practioners. I've also included a number of entries such as *social constructionism, reclaiming, gender identity* and *gay gene* which reflect recent developments in academic research into sexuality.

There are now arguably many more ways to be visibly gay or lesbian than in 1972 – *activists, A-gays, baby butches, bi-curios, ACT-UP clones, camp queens, closet-cases, daddies, drag-kings, ethical sluts, fag-hags, granola lesbians, gymbots, leather-men, lipstick lesbians, muscle bears, riot grrls, stone butches, strays, trannies* and *twinks* all testify to the proliferation of queer identities. These words may be viewed as types or (more frequently) stereotypes, but they and many more like them exist, with the possibility of being donned or shunned in different contexts. These identities don't have to be restraints, but can act as convenient roles, enabling them to be combined into continually changing hybrids. Or they can be ignored altogether – the 'I'm just me' identity being one of the loudest calls heard by many gay men and lesbians today.

As other gay lexicographers have found, the desire to find new words for sex and body parts related to sex continues to persist. Arguably, there is nothing essentially gay about a penis, but I've included lists of some of the more amusing terms for body parts for the sake of completeness. However, as this is a dictionary of terms that are used *by* gay men and lesbians, rather than terms that are used *on* them, I haven't spent too much time cataloguing the large number of derogatory words for homosexuals, many of which are created by non-homosexuals – in some cases there have been attempts to reclaim particular words and this has been noted. As far as I can tell, gay men and lesbians have always been much more cutting and witty when developing insults for each other and themselves, far surpassing any attempts made by bigots. So unsurprisingly, in the dictionary we find numerous words for types of people who are deemed irritating and/or unattractive: with the old (*corpse, granny, old girl, Peter Pan, troll*), the promiscuous (*baggage, bike, bitch in heat, slutbag, slapper, whorella*) and the ugly (*before shot, buffarilla, dog, mack truck, skag*) being more than adequately dealt with. As is also the case with the Polari dictionary, classifications according to masculinity and femininity (or effeminacy) continue to be seen as important (*final girl, stone butch, straight-acting, daddy, flamer, gym bunny, femme*).

Some of the most interesting sites of development in gay and lesbian slang have involved specialist, or marginalized groups: for example, the practice of *bare-backing* (anal sex without a condom) has resulted in the creation of a number of related slang terms (e.g. *bug-chaser, buzz load, charged cum, conversion party*) – the reconceptualization of bare-backing in the light of possible HIV infection and safe sex advice has made it one of the most controversial and taboo subjects within gay circles. *Bears* have also created fair-sized lexicons to name concepts and distinctions that are important and often unique to them (*arcotphile, cave, cub, grr, maul, otter*), as have *BDSM* practioners (*black hole, button pusher, collaring, gimp, head play, lifestyler*). Other types of gay slang have been collected from the genre of pornography (*fluffer, facial, nasty, money shot*), whereas the internet has also yielded a wide range of new phrases (*fubar, stats, damn tourist, cyber, m8, munch*), often used in gay chatrooms. Personal ads continue to evolve, throwing up new acronyms every year (*OHAC, PA, ALAWP, BND*) as tastes continue to change. Additionally, transgendered people (*drag kings* and *queens, female* and *male impersonators, transsexuals* and *transvestites*) have also contributed to the dictionary (*24 hour girl, skag drag, drab, black in white TV, butch striptease*).

Hagism has spawned a variety of related words. First there was the *fag-hag*: a (usually heterosexual) woman who had many gay friends. The meaning of the word *hag* has since shifted, from referring to women, to meaning anybody who has a particular attraction to another group: so we now have *drag-hags* (people who like drag queens), *hag-fags* (gay men with lots of female friends), *stag-hags* (people who like heterosexual men), *spag-hags,* (liking Italian men), *tag-hags* (those who like expensive designer clothing) and *trans-hags* (liking transgendered people).

As lexicographers like Donald Cory discovered in the

late 1960s, many gay slang words are ambivalent, reflecting two-sided feelings towards the speaker and hearer. Gay and lesbian slang may be many things: clever, funny, cruel, but politically correct it ain't. In compiling this dictionary I have taken care to include every word I came across, even if its meaning may offend certain groups – arguably the very existence of a gay dictionary is going to upset some people, so there's little point in being censorious when writing the book. However, I'd point out two important disclaimers – first, one should be careful of drawing too many conclusions about gay men and lesbians from the list of words, which are mostly taken out of context. Many of these terms are often used humorously, ironically or in self-deprecation. As a result, the 'sting' in many of these words is often lessened. Second, the dictionary shouldn't be considered as being representative of every member of every gay and lesbian community as a whole. During my research I found words which were only used by small groups of people. Other than being attracted to people from the same sex, there are no gay or lesbian universals (only stereotypes) and that includes language use. This dictionary should tell us something about the diversification and creativity of individual gay men and lesbians. It should *not* tell us about what makes us all the same.

DICTIONARY OF GAY SLANG

A

A noun: anal intercourse.

A2M verb: ass to mouth or **rimming**. Used in personal advertising slang.

AB+ adjective: antibody positive, testing positive for antibodies to **HIV**. *AB-* is antibody negative.

ABD adjective: acronym for *Attractive By Default*. In a room full of ugly people, an average-looking guy becomes *ABD*. From *The Broken Hearts Club* (2000).

Abigail noun: an abortion. From **Gayle**.

accordion noun: a penis which becomes exceptionally large when erect. 'I was so disappointed when he pulled down his pants. But then it was like, accordion time!'

active adjective: the inserter during anal intercourse. Also *boffer, fudge-packer, pitcher, porker, shit-stabber, top, top-man, topper, turd-burgler*. See **passive**.

active-passive split noun: the belief that in gay sex the person who gets fucked is feminine and somehow 'perverted' while the one doing the fucking still retains his masculine, 'normal' status.

activist noun: someone who tries to change an existing social or political order. See **direct action, zap action**.

ACT UP noun: acronym for *AIDS Coalition to Unleash Power*, a US direct action group founded by Michaelangelo

Signorile to fight the spread of **AIDS** and bring pressure on governments and other bodies to find a cure.

ACT UP clone, ACT UP queer noun: a late 1980s variant on the traditional **clone** who had very short hair, long sideburns, a clean shaven face, white t-shirt, Levi's and Doc Martens. The ACT UP clone is usually involved in numerous political causes. See **activist**.

Adam's pajamas adjective: naked.

Adonis noun: an attractive young man. From Greek mythology. Adonis was loved by the goddess Aphrodite. He ignored her advice and was killed while hunting a wild boar. Aphrodite persuaded the gods to let him come back to earth for six months of each year. She changed his blood into a flower, the anemone. Each year the blooming of the anemone signifies the return of Adonis from the underworld.

adult baby, AB noun: people who derive emotional and/ or erotic enjoyment from being dressed like and treated as a baby. Also *infantalist*.

after nines noun: closeted black gay men in South Africa who pretended to be heterosexual during the day, but 'come out' at night. From the book *Moffies* (2000) by Bart Luirink.

aftershock noun: feelings of shame, guilt or horror after participating in **BDSM** roleplay, especially as a **top**.

A-Gay noun: a gay man who possesses power, wealth or social standing. A-Gays are usually, but not always, white, middle-class and westernized. Used in Armistead Maupin's *More Tales of The City* (1980). 'The A-Gays could talk about whoever was tooting coke in the bathroom.' See also **power lesbian**.

agent provacateur noun: a plain-clothed police officer who attempts to entrap a gay man into having public sex. See also **pretty police**.

ageplay noun: a form of roleplay between two adult partners where one of them acts as a child or baby. In a small number of cases ageplay can extend to a lifestyle, with both partners remaining in the role all or most of the time.

AIDS noun: acronym for *Acquired Immune Deficiency Syndrome,* the most severe manifestation of **HIV** infection. A CD4+ T-Cell count below 200/mm^3 in addition to being HIV+ constitutes an AIDS diagnosis. AIDS gradually depletes the body's natural immune response system, resulting in it having little or no defence against opportunistic diseases. People with AIDS suffer from opportunistic infections and cancers, resulting in weight loss, diarrhoea, and a form of cancer called Karposi's sarcoma. A combination of anti–viral drugs can combat but not cure AIDS. At the time of writing there is no known cure.

AIDS terrorist noun: someone who is **HIV+** and knowingly engages in unsafe sex without telling his/her partners.

ALA acronym: gay personal advertising code for *All Letters Answered.*

ALAWP acronym: gay personal advert slang for *All Letters Answered With Photo* – any respondent who encloses a photograph will be guaranteed a reply. 'The ad said ALAWP, so why hasn't he replied to my letter?' 'Simple – you're ugly dear.'

alley apple noun: a shit.

analingus noun: the act of licking, tonguing, kissing and penetrating the anus with the tongue.

analismus noun: the failure of the anus to relax, preventing anal sex.

andro dyke noun: a lesbian who neither looks or acts particularly masculine or feminine.

androgynous adjective: someone whose sex is not apparent from their outward appearance. Also *brothersister*.

androtrope noun: a gay man. Coined by Kurt Hiller in 1946 who disliked the negative connotations of homosexual. See also **gynaeotrope**.

angel food noun: a gay man in the Air Force. US.

animal training noun: sexual roleplay in which one partner is an animal trainer and the other is the animal. Two of the most common types of animal training involve *ponyplay* and *dogplay*. Common fantasies can involve obedience training, exercise training, newspaper fetching, harnessing and riding etc. Other animal training roles include cats, tigers, pigs, cows and worms. Also *furrysex*.

anonymous sex noun: sex between two (or more) people who don't know each other.

anti-gay adjective: 1. a mode of thinking espoused in 1996 by openly gay writer Mark Simpson who edited a book of the same name. *Anti-gay* stood for people who were dissatisfied with certain aspects of the gay scene, for example its homogeneity, conformity, and obsession with youthful, muscular appearances. 2. a word sometimes used by **homophobes** to describe their personal stance.

APS noun: acronym for *Accurate Penis Size.*

APX verb: to give or to take strangulation or *erotic asphyxiation.* Advertising slang.

arctophile adjective: friendly towards **bear** culture.

armbreaker noun: an extremely energetic masturbation session.

arsehole noun: the anus. Also *a-hole,* **back door,** *blowhole, brown eye, cackpipe, chocolate starfish, chuff, chute, cornhole, crack, crapper, cum-hole, darkstar, dead eye, dirt track, dot, exhaust pipe, fuck hole, fudge pot, fudge tunnel, Gary Glitter, gash, Hershey highway, hole, hoop, jacksie, jam pot, leather, love channel, mangina, man-hole, man-pussy, marmite motorway, poop-chute, ring, ringpiece, rosebud, shit chute, shithole, shitter, slit, third eye, tradesman's entrance.*

Arthur adjective: 1. heterosexual. See also **Arthur or Martha**. 2. one who penetrates during anal intercourse. 3. noun: the act of masturbation. 'I had an arthur last night.' From Cockney rhyming slang: J. Arthur Rank (a British chain of cinemas) = wank.

Arthur or Martha adjective: unsure about sexuality or bisexual. 'That Bob doesn't know if he's Arthur or Martha.'

assistant top noun: someone who helps a **top** in **BDSM** or **D&S** roleplay. The assistant top may be younger or less experienced than the main top. Also *junior top, or top in training.*

attitude, 'tude noun: 1. sense of poise, a confident, sassy worldview. 1990s US slang. Madonna sings about 'ladies with an attitude' in her song *Vogue,* listing Bette Davis, Rita Hayworth, Ginger Rogers, Grace Kelly, Jean Harlow,

Katherine Hepburn, Lana Turner, Lauren Bacall, Greta Garbo and Marilyn Monroe as examples. Also the name of a UK gay magazine. 2. an air of superiority: 'He's cute, but he's got so much attitude it's not worth it.'

Aunt Jeminas noun: mid-1990s US nickname for gay Republicans who did little to prevent anti-gay initiatives by the religious right. The image of the original Aunt Jemina – plump and swathed in calico, was first used in 1893 in pancake syrup advertising campaigns. She has been seen as a stereotype of a black 'Mammy'.

Australian sex noun: sex involving licking, kissing and tonguing various parts of the body in the following order: the back of the neck and shoulders, down and up the spine, the back of neck and shoulders, the side of neck, mouth, bottom of spine, anus and beyond. This should take between 15 minutes to an hour. The person doing the licking is an *Australian active*, while the person being licked is an *Australian passive*. See **New Zealand sex**.

autofellatio noun: the act of sucking your own penis. About three per cent of men are able to do this. Also *self-suck*.

autosexual adjective: someone whose chief sexual outlet is masturbation.

B

B&D noun: acronym for bondage and discipline. A milder form of **S&M** which involves at least one partner being constrained. Pain is usually not involved and power roles are less defined than in S&M.

BA adjective: acronym for *bare-assed* (naked).

baa adjective: small. UK rare. 'He had such a baa cock that I couldn't tell if it was in or not.'

baby butch noun: a young or young-looking lesbian who acts **butch**.

baby dyke noun: a young and/or inexperienced lesbian.

babycakes noun: term of endearment, popularized in the Armistead Maupin *Tales of The City* novels.

bachelor noun: a synonym for *gay*.

back door noun: arsehole. 'Mark got his back door kicked again last night' means that Mark got fucked last night.

back door off the hinges noun: diarrhoea.

back room noun: a room (usually darkened and towards the back of a gay bar or club) where sexual activity takes place between patrons. Back rooms were popularized in the 1970s in the US. In the age of **AIDS**, back rooms are often equipped with *safer sex* items such as condoms and latex gloves. See also **dark room**.

bag noun: a promiscuous person.

bag boy noun: someone with an attractive body but an ugly face (which would need to be obscured by a bag before sex could take place). See **double bagger**.

baggage noun: 1. hang-ups or problems. 2. an insult, used to imply that someone is an old, promiscuous person.

bagging verb: a form of concealing a sexual partner in the cubicle of a public toilet during **cottaging** (see Polari entry) or **tea-room** sex, to avoid police detection. One man sits on the toilet while the other stands facing him, with a plastic bag pulled up around his feet. If a policeman looks under the gap at the bottom of the door, only one pair of feet will be seen.

bagpiping verb: making a small cut in the scrotum, inserting a straw into it and then blowing. The inflated scrotum sac is then sealed with a plaster, prior to sex.

bake and baste verb: to offer to rub suntan oil on someone's back, as part of a plan to fuck them.

ball-bearing stewardess noun: a male or **f-t-m** flight attendant.

balls noun: 1. testicles. Also *bags, diamonds, eggs, family jewels, gongs, goolies, happy sack, nads, nards, nuts, rocks, sack, stones*. 2. courage.

Bambi sexuality noun: sexual interaction based around touching, cuddling and kissing rather than genital contact or penetration.

banana noun 1. a curved penis. 2. an East Asian gay man who espouses western values and often prefers to have sex with Caucasians. 'Yellow on the outside, white on the inside.' Derogatory.

bar biography noun: 1. a personal or family history which is either exaggerated or revisionist. 2. a false or inflated view of oneself. From the phenomenon of trying to impress people in bars or clubs by lying about the details of your life. 'In Allan's bar biography he's the Queen of Spain.'

Barbara noun: a heterosexual man. From **Gayle**.

Barbie noun: a scatter-brained drag queen.

bareback, BB verb: to have anal sex with someone without using a condom. Barebacking developed in the late 1990s and has coincided with the availability of combination therapies which although they do not cure **AIDS** (and produce side effects including stomach cramps, nausea, vomiting, diarrhoea, headaches, fevers and fatigue), have been shown to raise the number of CD4 or T-cells, an index of how well the immune system is working. Barebacking is one of the most complex and controversial issues surrounding gay sexuality. Many gay men cannot understand why anyone would even consider it, others believe it is a matter of personal choice and for a minority, a subculture has developed around it. Also known as *apache*. See **barebacking party, bug-brothers, bug-chaser, buzz load, charged cum, conversion party, fuck of death, (the) gift, gift-giver, Russian roulette party**.

barebacking party noun: a group sex party where condoms are not used. Several types of barebacking parties exist – 1. all of the participants are HIV positive. 2. all of the participants are (supposed to be) HIV negative. 3. **conversion parties** 4. **Russian roulette parties**.

basher noun: someone who physically or verbally assaults homosexuals. Some bashers may operate in groups, hanging around cruising areas or outside gay bars or clubs, waiting for an opportunity to attack an isolated gay man. Others may engage in sex with a gay man and afterwards attack, rob or blackmail him.

basket noun: a man's crotch. Also *box*, **lunch**, *packet*.

basket days noun: periods of warm weather which allow men to wear light garments so that their baskets can be spotted under them.

basket shopping verb: to stare at men's crotches while in a public place. Also *basket picnic*. A person who engages in basket shopping is a *basketeer*.

basket weaver noun: a man who wears tight-fitting clothes and continually fondles his penis through them.

baths (the), bath-house noun: Turkish baths which were popular male cruising sites, particularly in the US in the 1970s, as well as places of entertainment and social interaction. In New York, popular bath-houses were Everards (where a fire killed nine patrons, similar to the incident in Larry Kramer's 1978 novel *Faggots*), Club Baths which operated its own venereal clinic for a time and The Continental where Bette Midler launched her career, and which was the inspiration behind the film *The Ritz* (1976). In the 1980s, many bath-houses were closed down as a direct result of **AIDS**, although some bath-houses in the US (e.g. the New St Marks) made the clientele sign an agreement or contract saying they would practice **safe sex**. The UK saw a significant number of bath-houses opening in the 1990s, being referred to as **gay saunas**. Also *the tubs, the vapours*.

bath sign language noun: non-verbal codes used in **bath-houses** or **gay saunas**. For example, knotting the towel at the back, or lying on one's stomach indicates you would like to be fucked. Lying on one's back on a cot with the legs spread apart means you want to receive oral sex.

BATS adjective: acronym for someone who is *Better Looking Across The Street*. Also *thirty-footer*. From *The Broken Hearts Club* (2000).

battyman, battyboy noun: gay man. From Afro-Carribbean slang. Derogatory.

BB noun: 1. a bodybuilder. verb: 2. to **bareback**.

BBBJ noun: acronym for *bareback blowjob* – oral sex without a condom. See also **bareback**.

BBM noun: a bisexual black male. From personal advertising slang.

b-boy noun: shortened version of *bottom boy* – a young man who likes to be fucked.

BDSM noun: umbrella term for **bondage, discipline** and *sado-masochism* (see **S&M**). A way of linguistically uniting different groups whose actual practices may differ.

be one of the knights verb: to have syphilis.

bean queen noun: a gay man who is attracted to Latino or Hispanic men. As with all similar terms (*potato queen, rice queen*) relating to certain types of men, they are often thought to be derogatory.

bear noun: a gay man who generally possesses one or more of the following traits: a hairy body, beard and/or moustache, large or tubby build, muscular development, masculine behaviour. Bears are usually older than twinks (although there are no age limits). Bear culture is a development of the **clone** look and a reaction against the dominant twentieth century ideal of gay male beauty as a **twink**. See **arctophile, bear chaser, bear code, behr, big bear, black bear, bruin, cave, cub, grizzly bear, grr, hirsute, koala bear, lace bear, leather bear, maul, muscle bear, otter, polar bear, ursine, ursophile, woof, wolf**.

bear chaser noun: a gay man who is sexually attracted to **bears**.

bear code noun: slang for *The Natural Bear Classification System*, developed by Bob Donahue and Jeff Stoner. The system uses punctuation, letters and numbers which allows a **bear** to describe himself and other bears. The initial code B is followed by a number from 0–9, showing beard-type: 0=no beard, 9=ZZ-top beard. Other letters are followed by positive (+ or ++) or negative (– or – –) signs that are used to strengthen or negate a particular trait e.g.: c: **cub** factor, d: **daddy** factor, e: endowment (penis size), f: fur (amount of body hair), g: grope (amount one likes to touch and be touched), k: kinky, l: leather, m: muscularity, p: peculiarities (idiosyncrasies), q: queenliness (camp or effeminacy), r: ruggedness (likes the outdoors), s: sex (or slut), t: tallness, w: weight. Additional punctuation includes v: variable trait, question mark: a guess, colon: observed but uncertain, exclamation mark: a trait is close to being a prototype – e.g. someone who had the largest penis ever would be e++!, brackets: for showing cross-overs or ranges e.g. w(++) suggests a bear whose weight fluctuates between merely tubby and obese. Visit the official web site at www.bearcode.com for more information. See also **grrl code**, **twink code**.

beard noun: a woman who is romantically paired with a gay man, allowing him to keep his sexuality hidden from the rest of the world. Like facial hair, a beard enables the man to appear more stereotypically 'male'. Beards were (and still are) popular accessories of closeted Hollywood stars. 'Have you seen Rock Hudson's latest beard? It's Liberace!' See also **frock**.

beard cover noun: make-up used by male **cross-dressers** to minimize the appearance of a beard shadow.

beat off verb: to masturbate. Also *beat, beat the meat.*

(the) beats noun: public toilets, especially where gay sex occurs. Australian slang.

beauty boy noun: an attractively feminine young man.

beef noun: men with muscles. Also *beefcake.*

beefcake magazine noun: a magazine, typically from the 1950s–1970s of clean-cut, muscular men posing in jock-straps.

beehive boy noun: a **drag queen** (of any age) who enjoys wearing beehive wigs.

before shot noun: an unattractive person who would benefit from a makeover. The term refers to 'before' and 'after' photos used to advertise miracle diets, hair restorer, plastic surgery etc.

behr noun: a **bear**-like man who can't or doesn't grow a beard, but does have a moustache.

beige adjective: boring, bland, neutral.

being read verb: when a **cross-dresser** is recognized by a member of the public as not belonging to the sex which he/she is dressed as. Also known as *getting clocked.*

bell end noun: the glans of the penis. Also *policeman's helmet, purple helmet.*

belle of the ball noun: a gay man who enjoys being the centre of attention.

bent stick noun: a penis which is unable to become erect.

berdache noun: a man or woman in American Indian cultures who is unwilling or unable to fit into the gender role assigned to his or her sex.

bf noun: boyfriend.

b-girl noun: a butch lesbian.

BHM noun: acronym for *Big Handsome Man* or *Bi Hispanic Male.*

BHR adjective: acronym for *Below Height Requirement* – someone who is attractive but too short. From *The Broken Hearts Club* (2000).

bi-curious adjective: a (usually heterosexual) person who has never had a gay or lesbian experience but wouldn't shut out the possibility in the future. 'That Susie reckons she's bi-curious, I say it's just a fashion statement.'

biffy noun: public toilets, especially where gay sex occurs. Canadian slang.

big bear noun: a chubby or large **bear**.

big girl noun: a gay man who attempts to be butch, but humorously fails. Also *big Mary, big 'mo, big woman.*

bi-kinky adjective: someone who is heterosexual during **vanilla**, penetrative sex, but willing to take same-sex partners during **S&M** roleplay.

binding verb: the act of taping down a female's breasts so that they are hidden underneath clothing. This is usually practiced by **f-t-m pre-op transsexuals**.

biological female/male noun: refers to sex at birth.

bi-phobia noun: an irrational hatred or fear of bisexuality.

bi-possible adjective: someone who is heterosexual during **vanilla**, penetrative sex, but may, in a power dynamic, be willing to take same-sex partners or explore bisexual scenarios.

biscuit game noun: a game played among all-male groups (usually consisting of heterosexual (or closeted) men or youths), the object being to masturbate in a circle over a biscuit. Everyone is required to shoot their cum onto the biscuit and the last person to do this has to eat it. Also called *sticky biscuit*. See **circle jerk**.

bi-serious adjective: a person who is definitely **bisexual**, as opposed to other states of bisexuality e.g. **bi-curious**, **bi-possible**.

bisexual, bi adjective: a person who is attracted to members of either sex. Also *AC-DC, Betty Bothways, double-gated, fence-jumper, switch-hitter*. See **bi-curious, bi-kinky, bi-possible, bi-serious**.

bitch 1. noun: a feminine or gay man. 2. noun: someone who is a **bottom** sexually. 3. verb: to complain. Used as early as 1000 BC in the form of *bicce*, the word originally referred to a female dog, and started being applied to women in about the fifteenth century.

bitch in heat noun: a gay man who is always desperate to have sex.

bitch's Christmas noun: Hallowe'en. Also *amateur night*.

bite the nails verb: any coded gesture to signify that a gay man is interested in making contact with another. Also *flag*.

biz noun: heterosexual sex.

black bear noun: a **bear** who is also black or African/American.

black hole noun: derogatory name for an uncommunicative or unresponsive **bottom** in **BDSM** roleplay.

black in white TV noun: a white **drag queen** or **transvestite** who adopts black culture and slang as her frame of reference.

black party noun: a party, usually held at a gay leather club, where only people wearing black clothing (preferably made of leather) may attend.

black triangle noun: a symbol in the form of an inverted triangle adopted by lesbians in remembrance of 'undesirables' (prostitutes, the mentally ill, and possibly lesbians) who were imprisoned in Nazi concentration camps. See also **pink triangle**.

blade slut noun: a person who derives sexual gratification from knives (but not necessarily from being cut by them).

blanket party noun: a prison beating or rape, using a blanket to smother and restrain the victim.

bless! vocative: used in a slightly patronizing, 'caring' way to evaluate someone's behaviour. 'Did you see Julie's karaoke rendition of *Baby Hit Me One More Time* last night? Bless!' UK.

blood sports noun: extreme **S&M** play which involves cutting and piercing the skin, or any other activity which deliberately draws blood.

blow job noun: fellatio. Also *brush one's teeth, chow down, cock suck, deep throat, dick lick, draw the blinds, draw the curtains, eat, eat it, eat the meat, face fuck, French, girth and mirth, give head, gob job, gob the knob, go down, gum, gunch, head job, hummer, lunch, munch, nosh, pickle chugging, skull, smoke the big one, suck cock, tongue job.*

blow out the plug verb: to defecate after being penetrated anally.

blue adjective: 1. pornographic e.g. a blue movie. 2. gay. 3. noun: the idea that homophobia would end if everyone who was gay or bisexual turned blue overnight, or had a blue dot on their forehead.

blue balls noun: the need to experience orgasm, often after being sexually stimulated for a long period of time.

BND noun: acronym for *Boy Next Door*. Used in personal adverts.

BOB noun: acronym for *Battery Operated Boyfriend* referring to a **vibrator**.

bod noun: a person who has an attractive body.

BOD noun: acronym for *Box of Death,* to describe someone who is **well-hung**.

body modification noun: umbrella name for a collection of practices such as tattooing, branding, corseting, piercing, binding, scarification or anything that people do in order to alter some aspect of their body. Also *bod mod* or *mod.*

body service noun: sexual roleplay where a **sub** or **bottom** takes care of a **top**'s bodily and hygiene needs, such as bathing, shaving, hair-styling, manicuring, massage, pedicures etc.

body worship noun: sexual roleplay where a **sub** or **bottom** kisses, sucks and licks any part of a **top**'s body, without inhibitions.

bog queen noun: a man who frequents public toilets for sex. UK. Also *cottage queen, privy queen.*

boi noun: 1. a young, usually cute, gay man. US 2. a lesbian **bottom** in **BDSM** roleplay.

bonch noun: the perineum, the area between the base of a man's testicles and his anus.

bondage noun: a form of erotic play which involves one (or more) partners tying up or restraining another or others. Bondage is often linked with **discipline**. See **BDSM.**

bone smuggler noun: a **drag queen**. US.

boobs noun: female breasts. Also *bazooms, dirty pillows, honkers, hooters, jugs, knockers, lemons, mams, maracas, melons, piggies, puppies, rack, set, shakers, tits, titties, udders.*

boot boy noun: a submissive gay man who has a fetish for leather boots worn by **tops**. Boot boys may work at a leather bar or will shine shoes at a charitable event. See also **foot worship**.

booty noun: 1. the **bottom**. 2. sex. US.

born again virgin noun: someone who used to be a bit of a **slut** but has since given up sex. Also *secondary virgin.*

bosch verb: to drill a **glory hole** or peephole between two toilet stalls, for the purposes of cottaging.

bossy bottom noun: a gay man who enjoys being the passive partner in anal sex, but likes to completely control the experience. 'Tom's such a bossy bottom that my cock was in traction for a week after I fucked him!'

Boston marriage noun: two lesbians living together. A nineteenth century New England term.

bottom noun: 1. the buttocks. Also *arse, ass, azz, backside, behind, booty, box, bum, buns, butt, buttocks, cheeks, coochie, fanny, glutes, pooper, rear, sweet-cheeks, tail, tooshie, tush.* 2. a gay man who prefers to be the passive partner during anal intercourse. See **passive**. 3. a submissive person during sado-masochistic or bondage and domination rolepay. Easton and Liszt in *The Topping Book* (1995: 5) define a *bottom* as referring to 'slaves, masochists, submissives, doggies, horsies, captives, "kids", victims and other receptive parties'.

bottomless pit noun: 1. a state of consciousness during **BDSM** roleplay where a **bottom** is enjoying the scene so much that he/she wants it to continue forever. Also called *The Forever Place.* In this state, the bottom is unable to make informed consent, placing responsibility of judgement on the **top**. 2. an insatiable **bottom**.

box 1. a woman's vagina. 2. the anus or bottom. 3. a man's crotch area.

boy noun: 1. a male **bottom** in the **BDSM** sense who roleplays being young. 2. a boyish lesbian. Also *boydyke*. 3. a young gay man.

boyfriend noun: a gay male sexual partner. See **girlfriend**.

boy toy noun: a young gay man (usually aged between 18–21), often wearing tight or revealing club-wear.

boyz noun: plural of **boy**, also the name of a UK gay listings paper.

breadboard noun: a board used to present the male genitals for **CBT**.

breath control noun: a form of **edgeplay** where a **bottom**'s ability to breathe is restricted by a **top**, either by placing constrictions around the neck or blocking the mouth or nose. This is done for extremely tiny amounts of time and rarely to the point of unconciousness.

breeder noun: a somewhat derogatory description of heterosexuals, focussing on their propensity to have children.

bring off verb: to cause someone to achieve orgasm.

bring out verb: 1. to enable someone to be honest about their sexuality. 2. refers to an older, more experienced gay man initiating a younger gay man into a sexual relationship for the first time.

bronco noun: a young man who is difficult to restrain during sex.

brown noun: a sexual fetish for faeces.

Brown family (the) noun: the gay subculture.

brown shower noun: the act of defecating on someone for sexual enjoyment. See also **golden shower**.

brownie queen noun: the **bottom** in anal sex. A *brownie king* is a **top** in anal sex.

browning verb: anal sex. Also *brown-hatter, brown holing, brown job.*

bruin noun: a **bear** who is athletic and particularly likes contact sports.

BSO noun: acronym for *Bisexual Significant Other*. See **significant other**.

bubble-butt noun: a particularly muscular and well-rounded bottom. A *butt-boy* is a young man with a rounded, muscular bottom who likes to be fucked.

bubble-yum noun: someone who has a **bubble-butt**.

bucket bum noun: an arse which is extremely accustomed to being fucked. Also *grit required, Slack Alice.*

buddy noun: 1. a volunteer who helps a **PLWA** with everyday household tasks, shopping etc. as well as being a companion and friend. 2. a penis.

buddy booth noun: booths in an adult movie theatre, book or video store which have individual video screens. By inserting a coin in a slot, for a limited amount of time a fixed screen between two booths will raise, revealing a window, so two men in adjacent booths will be able to see each other.

buff, buffed adjective: muscular or pumped up after exercise. US slang.

buffarilla noun: a large and/or unattractive woman. Also *boiler, dog, horse-face, mack truck, moose, ogress, skag.*

buffet noun: 1. a man who is the central focus of attention during an orgy. 2. a smorgasbord of sexual possibilities: straight, gay, group sex etc. Originates from the term *buffet flat,* an apartment that gay men and lesbians would retire to after the bars had closed in Harlem in the 1920s.

bug-brothers noun: a group of **HIV** positive men. From **barebacking** slang.

bug-chaser, BC noun: a man who wants to become infected with **HIV**. From **barebacking** slang.

bukkake noun: derived from the Japanese word meaning heavy splash or squirt, *bukkake* is a term found in pornography involving one person receiving multiple **facials** from numerous males. While the original bukkake films featured Japanese women, the term has crossed over into gay pornography.

bull, bull dagger noun: a lesbian, especially a masculine one. From early twentieth century slang *bull dogger*: a black cowgirl, or black lesbian. Also *butch dagger*. See **bull dyke**.

bull dyke noun: a masculine, strong lesbian. Also *boon-dagger, bull, bullbitch, dykosaurus*. See also **bull dagger**.

bull's balls noun: large testicles, thought to be a sign of virility.

bum 1. noun: buttocks and/or anus. 2. verb: to fuck someone anally. UK. 'The first time anyone bummed me it hurt like hell.' The terms *bumboy, bumchum* and *bummer* were popular UK schoolboy insults for *homosexuals* in the late twentieth century.

bump and twirl verb: to party.

bum pusher noun: a 'heterosexual' man who goes cruising for **rent boys**. UK.

bunce adjective: rounded or clumpy. UK rare. The opposite of **pince**.

bungie boy noun: a young, **straight-acting** gay or **bisexual** man.

bunker shy noun: a young man who is afraid of being forced into having (usually institutionalized) gay sex. Originates from nineteenth century prison slang.

bunny fuck noun: a very quick sexual act.

bush noun: pubic hair. Also *fuzz, pubes, thatch.*

busy adjective: 1. flamboyant. 2. to be in pursuit of a sexual partner.

butch 1. adjective: aggressively masculine. *Butch* is most likely taken from early twentieth century US slang; the crewcut hairstyle was also known as a *butch-cut*. It is also a colloquial abbreviation of *butcher* – itself seen as a masculine, aggressive trade. The nickname 'Butch' was given to tough men as early as 1902 e.g. 'Butch' Cassidy. *Butch* can be applied to both males and females (a butch woman is usually a lesbian) but is usually a positive evaluatory term when used to describe a man. Inness and

Lloyd (1996: 11), in their discussion of lesbian 'butch', note that:

> . . . 'butch' is an important word in the gay male lexicon, with multiple meanings. Employed as a campy adjective, 'Oh isn't Brian looking butch today!', the word has a light-hearted tone; on the other end of the spectrum are the gay men who take their butch identity very seriously, labouring endlessly to achieve and maintain the most masculine physique, bearing and overall presence.

2. noun: a *butch* can be used to refer to a masculine acting man or lesbian.

butchilinity noun: the trait of butchness.

butch it up verb: to attempt to act more masculine, either to make others laugh, to conceal one's sexuality or to appear more attractive.

butchophobia noun: a fear and/or hatred of masculine women.

butch sister noun: a heterosexual man.

butch striptease noun: a striptease performed by a **drag king** who takes off enough clothes to reveal the female body underneath.

butterfly queen noun: a gay man who likes to **sixty nine**.

butt floss noun: the hair around the anus.

button pusher noun: an intense **BDSM** scene which is likely to provoke extreme emotional conflict – for example, one which involves abandonment, humiliation, regression to child or baby states or anger.

butt plug noun: a toy which is inserted into the anus for sexual pleasure.

butt-ramming verb: aggressive anal sex.

buzz load noun: the experience of a 'rush' or high when receiving either what is known to be, or may possibly be **HIV**-infected semen (usually during anal sex). **Barebacking** slang.

BWM adjective: acronym for *Bisexual White Male.*

byke noun: a bisexual dyke.

C

cabin fever noun: a heterosexual man's willingness to settle for gay sex when he has been confined in all male company for a long period of time. Also *lost at sea.* Both terms originate from the prevalence of discreet homosexual relationships in the Navy.

camp, campy 1. adjective (also noun, verb): flamboyantly effeminate, original, amusing, homosexual, affected. Originally used at the beginning of the twentieth century. Possibly derived from the acronym *KAMP*: 'Known As Male Prostitute'. *Camp* is notoriously difficult to define, partly because it is a broad concept, connected to taste, sensibility, humour, parody, class, homosexuality and effeminacy, and because attitudes towards it have changed considerably over time. As Ross (1989: 146) notes, 'universal definitions of camp are rarely useful'.

2. Camp is often used with reference to the humour or style of effeminate, witty men. However, over-stated masculinity can also be camp – for example, many of the stylized **beefcake** magazines featuring muscular men posing in jockstraps are now considered to be camp. Sontag (1966: 279) viewed camp as 'a certain form of aestheticism,' evaluating objects 'not in terms of Beauty, but in terms of degree of artifice or stylization'. For Sontag, camp was playful, detached and apolitical. However, according to Ross (1993: 74) camp can be seen as a form of *cultural economy*. 'It challenged . . . legitimate definitions of taste and sexuality. But we must also remember to what extent this cultural economy was tied to the capitalist logic of development that governed the mass culture industries.'

Long (1993: 78) argues that camp is a 'moral activity'. For gay men who have been ridiculed because of their sexuality, their tragedy becomes trivial. Camp allows them to respond by taking the trivial seriously, 'parodying the forces of oppression' (Long 1993: 79).

Meyer (1994: 1) redefines camp again – as 'political and critical'. Casting aside the notion that camp is merely a 'sensibility', Meyer casts camp as a 'solely queer discourse' (1994: 1) and 'the total body of performative practices and strategies used to enact a queer identity, with enactment defined as the production of social visibility' (1994: 5). Medhurst (1997: 281) disagrees: 'Meyer's excessive claims for camp as always-and-only-radical cannot convince anyone who has spent time among camp queens, whose turns of phrase and ideological outlook can be frighteningly reactionary.'

camp it up verb: to act flamboyantly **camp** or effeminate. 'You should have seen Luke – one vodka and tomato juice and he's camping it up something rotten to The Village People.'

camp name noun: the renaming of a gay man (or in

some cases a lesbian) with an opposite-sex name. These names may be used to describe a particular physical or personality trait possessed by the person, based on stereotypes associated with the name – for example a shy or unattractive gay man may be rechristened as *Doris*, *Maureen* or *Mavis*. A more glamorous gay man could be called *Gloria* or *Marilyn*. Sometimes camp names can be used ironically or sarcastically – so an unglamorous name like *Hilda* may be applied to a particularly vain gay man. In other cases, the name may be expanded to describe a particular attribute: *Threeway Mary* (one who is renowned for having threesome sex), *The Black Widow* (a spiteful gay man who wears black clothing), *Fishy Franny* (a gay sailor). Finally, a camp name may be assigned on an alliterative basis, retaining the first letter of a person's real name. So *Harold Robbins* could become either *Harriet* or *Rita Robbins*. See also **drag queen name**.

candy ass noun: description of a young, attractive, slightly nelly gay man. US.

carpet licker noun: one who performs cunnilingus.

caspering verb: to attempt to simulate sex with someone who has passed out from drinking too much. From the movie *Kids* (1995) where this manoeuvre occurs, following the phrase 'Don't worry, it's just me – Casper'.

catcher noun: see **passive**.

cave, bear cave noun: any place where **bears** socialize.

CBT noun: acronym for *Cock and Ball Torture*. Used in **S&M** roleplay and also found in personal advert or internet chatroom slang. Refers to sadistic play with the male genitals, usually with leather bindings.

CBTT noun: acronym for *Cock, Ball and Tit Torture*. See also **CBT, tit torture**.

change your luck verb: 1. to have gay sex for the first time. 2. to have sex with a black person for the first time.

chapeau du chance noun: psuedo-French for *lucky hat*. A baseball cap or similar worn by a bald or balding gay man while cruising, in order to improve his luck. UK rare.

chapstick lesbian noun: a lesbian who enjoys playing sports.

charged cum, poz cum noun: the semen of an **HIV** positive man. **Barebacking** slang.

CHE noun: In the UK the *Campaign for Homosexual Equality* (CHE) which began in 1954 as the North-Western Committee for Homosexual Law Reform had many similar goals to the **Mattachine Society**.

Chelsea boy noun: a muscular **twink** with hardly any body fat, a shaved body and face and lots of **attitude**. US slang.

chem-friendly adjective: likes to do drugs.

Cherry Grove noun: a summer beach resort on **Fire Island** which was founded in the late nineteenth century.

cherry queen noun: a gay man who likes to initiate virgins.

chicken-hawk noun: one who prefers to have sex with young men. The wealthy American widow played by Vivien Leigh in the film *The Roman Spring of Mrs Stone*

(1961) is mockingly called a chicken-hawk for her relationship with the character played by a very young Warren Beatty. Also *chicken queen*, **fox**.

chockie nose noun: a **homoerotic**, **S&M**, **scat**-based fraternity house game involving groups of drunken heterosexual males. One member of the group is held down while another removes his underwear and then lowers himself onto the victim's face, with the intent of leaving a brown stain on his nose. This is referred to as a chockie (chocolate) nose. See also **biscuit game**.

chub adjective: short for chubby. Synonymous with *bulk*. The chub subculture exists within the gay subculture. See also **bear**, **chub envy**, **encourager**, **gainer**, **lineman**.

chub envy noun: the desire to be **chub**, or for one's partner to be chub.

church noun: bath-house. US slang.

ciao vocative: Italian for *hello* or *goodbye*. A (mock-) sophisticated way of saying *goodbye* in US gay slang.

cigar boy noun: a gay man who has a sexual fetish for **cigar daddies** and **pipe men**.

cigar daddy noun: a masculine, usually mature man (similar in some ways to a **bear**) who smokes cigars as a sexual fetish. Cigar daddies may allow others to watch or **body worship** them while they smoke cigars. See **pipe man**.

circle noun: the close friends and other social contacts of a gay man or lesbian.

circle jerk noun: group masturbation (or in some cases mutual masturbation). US. See also **biscuit game**.

circuit noun: the annual string of gay dance parties in the US including the White Parties, Black Party, Hotlanta and the GMHC Morning Party.

circuit queen noun: a gay man who lives for the **circuit**.

clap clinic noun: a genito-urinary clinic. UK.

Clause 28 noun: a UK legal clause, coined under Margaret Thatcher's Conservative goverment which since 1988 forbade local authorities to 'intentionally promote homosexuality' or 'promote the teaching in any maintained school the acceptability of homosexuality as a pretended family relationship'. Clause 28 was repealed in Scotland on 21st June 2000, despite a well-funded *Keep The Clause* campaign, backed by Stagecoach bus company owner Brian Souter and Cardinal Winning. Also known as *Section 28, Section 2A*. See **scrap the clause, direct action**.

clean adjective: 1. not having any sexually transmitted diseases. 2. to have not taken drugs. The acronym *d/d* used in personal advertising slang stands for *drug/disease free*.

clean queen noun: a gay man who always wears ironed shirts, brushes his hair and is obsessed with keeping his home tidy, continually dusting, wiping down work surfaces, picking bits of dirt off the carpets and fretting if anybody spills a drink on his sofa.

clear adjective: completely gay or lesbian.

clear the custard verb: to masturbate after having abstained from any form of sex for a long time.

clientele verb: to have sex. **Drag queen** slang.

clipper party noun: a party attended by men who have a fetish for shaving hair, particularly because of its military/masculine connotations. Some clipper parties are merely hair-shaving parties, but others can involve sex.

clock verb: 1. to recognize that someone is **transgendered**. 2. to attempt to make eye contact with someone.

clone noun: one of the first masculine gay identities of the 1970s, clones were so-called because of their homogenous and easily recognizable look. This included a moustache, short hair, check shirt and denim jeans. Clones were especially associated with the gay scene in San Francisco, hence the term *Castro clone*, referring to the Castro area which had become established as the centre of the city's gay scene.

clone zone 1. a place where large amounts of **clones** are found. 2. the name of a UK gay retail shop.

closet noun: the status of a gay man or lesbian who is yet to declare their sexuality. Most likely from the American idiom *skeleton in the closet* meaning a secret, although the word has become widened to refer to other forms of secrecy: 'I've found all these photos of William Shatner – please tell me you're a closet Star Trek fan!'

closet case, closet queen noun: someone who is unable to admit their sexuality either to themselves or to others, despite the fact that other people have already guessed. Also *crushed fruit, hidden queen*.

club kid noun: a gay man who goes to gay bars or nightclubs on a weekly (or daily) basis.

clutch your pearls verb: 1. the unconscious act of grasping for a string of imaginary pearls round the neck during a moment of tension. 2. to become upset or worked up.

cock noun: the penis. Also *arm, baloney, banger, blue-veined porridge gun, bone phone, buddy, bush-whacker, butcher knife, chopper, chutney ferret, dick, dobber, dong, donger, donkey, earthworm, enchilda, flesh pencil, fuck muscle, fuckpole, gigglestick, glory pole, gob-stopper, hair-splitter, hairy sausage, hambone, head, horn, ice-cream machine, jammy, jimmy, Johnson, joystick, kickstand, knob, knockwurst, lipstick, loaded gun, love gun, love muscle, love truncheon, lung disturber, meat, milkman, moisture missile, mutton bayonet, nudger, oboe, one-eyed Cyclops, pecker, peter, pipe, plonker, poker, popsicle, pork sword, prick, privates, pulse, rod, salty yoghurt, schlong, shit-stick, slinger, stick of rock, sticky spud gun, swack, sweetmeat, third leg, todger, tool, trouser snake, wang-tang, whammer, willy, yang, yoyo, zipperfish.*

cock cheese noun: the build-up of smegma around the head of an unwashed penis.

cock ring noun: a metal ring or leather strap which can be secured around the base of an erect penis and testicles, blocking the flow of blood and therefore enhancing an erection. Also *napkin ring,* See **three gates of hell**.

cock sucker noun: 1. someone who performs oral sex on a man. Also *cannibal, man-eater, suck queen.* 2. a derogatory term for any gay man.

cock sucker red adjective: the perfect shade of lipstick. **Drag queen** slang, quoted in Darrin Hagen's *The Edmonton Queen* (1997).

collaring verb: a **BDSM** ceremony where a **sub** formally accepts the collar of a **dom** and becomes officially 'owned'.

This ceremony is equivalent to a wedding and would be witnessed by friends and other members of the BDSM scene.

colourful TV, colour TV noun: a **drag queen** or **transvestite** who likes to wear flamboyant, attention-getting clothes.

come noun: semen (see **cum**). verb: to orgasm. Also *blast off, blow a load, blow one's juice, bust a nut, fire a shot, get nut, get one's rocks off, make it, pop, pop one's cork, shoot, shoot a load, shoot a wad.*

come bustin' over verb: to arrive at someone's place, uninvited and unwelcome. **Drag queen** slang.

come out verb: to openly declare your sexuality to others. Derived from the phrase *come out of the closet.* A study by Gregory Herek and John Capitanio published in *Personality and Social Psychology Bulletin* (1996) found that heterosexuals tend to hold more favourable attitudes about homosexuality if they know two or more gay people who are close friends or immediate family members and if there has been open discussion about the person's sexual orientation. Also *debut.* See also **closet, out**.

coming out story noun: a personal narrative which can involve one or more of the following elements: realizing one's sexuality for the first time, first gay or lesbian sexual experience, telling friends or family about sexuality or being discovered involuntarily as gay or lesbian.

commitment ceremony noun: a public affirmation of a relationship between a same-sex couple.

community (the) noun: a blanket term for a particular scene e.g. the gay and lesbian community, the cross-dressing community, the **BDSM** community. Includes bars and clubs, educational outreach groups, social clubs, support groups and other organizations.

con noun: consensual sex. Internet slang.

condom noun: a device made of latex rubber, designed to prevent the exchange of seminal fluid during sex, which can result in pregnancy or the transmission of diseases and viruses such as **HIV**, hepatitis, gonorrhoea, syphilis etc. While not 100% failsafe, they are used as part of anal, vaginal and oral safer sex practices. Water-based lubricants should be used with condoms as oil-based lubricants can damage them. Also *blob, cum-drum, French letter, Johnson cover, life jacket, love-glove, prophylactic, raincoat, rubber, rubber johnny, sleeve, weiner wrap*. See **rubber up, safe sex.**

connie noun: cocaine.

console TV noun: a **transvestite** or **drag queen** who is overweight.

control queen noun: someone who wants to take charge of every situation.

conversion noun: a person who wants to become **HIV** positive. **Barebacking** slang.

conversion party, sero-conversion party noun: a group sex party where **HIV** negative men allow themselves to become infected by HIV positive men. **Barebacking** slang.

convertible noun: 1. someone who can alternate between **top** and **bottom** roles (see **switch**). 2. someone who is bisexual.

cookies (the) noun: anal sex. US gay hip-hop/rap slang. See **homie-sexual**. 'I won't give the cookies to any faggot, he has to have a wife or girlfriend.'

cornholing verb: to have anal sex. US. A *cornholer* is the inserter.

corpse noun: a very old man who pesters much younger guys for sex.

cosmetic effect of distance, CED noun: the effect of distance and/or 'sympathetic lighting' which makes a person look more attractive than they really are. 'Across the bar he looked like Tom Cruise, but when I got up close the CED wore off and I realized he was an old girl in a toupee.'

cotton kid noun: a generic-looking, reasonably attractive guy who buys all of his clothes from J-Crew, Gap and Banana Republic. US slang.

cover girl noun: a **drag queen** or **transvestite** who looks attractive in drag or is secretive about her alternative gender identity.

CP noun: acronym for *Corporal Punishment*.

cross-dresser, CD noun: a person who wears clothes and acts as a member of the opposite sex, usually for emotional or sexual gratification. Also *X-dresser*, **transvestite**.

cruise verb: to look for sex. *Cruise* originated in the sixteenth century and was first used in connection with the movement of ships in the sea. By the end of the seventeenth century, its meaning had generalized to other types of movement, including people:

'Madam, how would you like to cruise about a little':
Farquhar, Love and Bottle, 1698
(Cited in *Oxford English Dictionary*, 1994).

However, the gay meaning of *cruise*, most likely comes from twentieth century North America, where it was used to mean walking or driving around, either aimlessly, or to look for casual sex (especially gay) partners. In *Tearoom Trade* (1970), Laud Humphreys describes how cruising was a popular activity for gay men as a result of the popularity of the automobile and the installation of a comprehensive water system across American towns, which preceded the creation of a number of public conveniences in secluded areas in parks.

As well as the 'movement' use of cruise, the word can also be used to describe the intense, interested way that a man looks at a potential sexual partner: 'I've been cruised at least five times since leaving the house this morning.' See **sticky eye contact**.

crunt noun: a woman who dislikes gay men – derived from a combination of *crone* and *cunt*. Derogatory.

crystal dick noun: impotence caused by taking drugs such as cocaine or amphetamines.

cub noun: a young **bear**, or one who is shorter and/or lacks other traditional bear elements (e.g. no beard). May also refer to a submissive or inexperienced bear.

cum 1. verb: to orgasm (see **come**). 2. noun: semen. Also *axle grease, baa liquids, baby gravy, beef gravy, chism, cock snot, come juice, cream, dick-splash, duck butter, face cream, gism, gravy, honey, hot milk, jizz, joy juice, load, love custard, man juice, man's milk, mess, pearl, pecker tracks, slime, snot, spooge, spunk, wad, whipped cream.*

cum bubble noun: a generic insult.

cum control noun: the act of repeatedly bringing someone to near-orgasm.

cum rag noun: 1. a handkerchief, towel, piece of tissue paper or clothing used to mop up **cum** after sex. 2. a gay man who is sexually passive and enjoys having lots of men cum on him.

curious adjective: advertising slang for someone who is inexperienced at gay or lesbian sex. Also *first-timer, novice.*

curry queen noun: someone who is sexually attracted to Asian or Indian men. Derogatory.

cut adjective: 1. circumcized. Also *helmet, kosher, low neck and short sleeves, peeled queen.* 2. having well-defined muscles. Also *ripped.*

cute daddy noun: an attractive man who has children. Also *pretty hot daddy, PHD.*

cut sleeves noun: pertaining to homosexuality. Derived from the Chinese story of Emperor Ai-ti (6 BC to 2 AD) who cut off the sleeves of his robe, rather than disturb his lover, who had fallen asleep on them.

cutter noun: someone who is willing to perform a castration.

cyber noun: cybersex – sex-talk in internet chatrooms.

cybersissy noun: someone who takes on a femme or female identity while using the internet, even though they are male or butch in real life.

D

D&S noun: acronym for *Dominance and Submission*. Also known as *power-relationships* and related to **BDSM**. Can be used to refer to any relationship where one person is sexually dominant and another is submissive. See **power exchange**.

daddy noun: 1. an older, generally masculine gay man who usually takes the active, dominant or caring role: 'Who's your Daddy?' 2. anyone who assumes a paternal or mentoring role with a submissive in **BDSM** roleplay or expresses a masculine identity. Therefore, daddies do not have to be male – lesbian, bi and heterosexual women can take a daddy role. However, the terms *mommy* or *daddi* can also be used as female equivalents of *daddy*.

dairy queen noun: a gay man who likes to suck or chew on his partner's nipples.

daisy chain noun: group sex activity where several people are linked together, usually via oral sex. A *closed daisy chain* involves a circle of group sex, where the first person is fucked or sucked by the last.

dark room noun: similar to a **back room** (but generally in total darkness), dark rooms can also be found in some **bath-houses** or **gay saunas** as well as bars.

dash noun: snogging or making out. UK. See also **dot**. 'So how was last night with Tom? Oh you know, dot, dot, dot, dash, dash, DASH!'

date 1. verb: to go out with someone. 2. noun: a companion to a social event. 3. noun: a sexual partner, used in the same way as **trick**. US.

date face noun: an unconscious facial expression a person assumes when he/she is attracted to someone.

datette noun: a short date, usually without an overnight stay. See also **fuck date**.

Daughters of Bilitis noun: one of the earliest organized, political lesbian groups, formed in 1955 by Del Martin and Phyllis Lyon.

day without art noun: on 1st December, to commemorate World AIDS Day, many cultural institutions, galleries and museums close their doors or drape works of art in memory of those who have died of **AIDS**.

DDG adjective: acronym for *Drop Dead Gorgeous*, someone who is very attractive.

delish adjective: delicious.

denim scene noun: a subculture whose members prefer to wear denim jeans, shirts and jackets. Often associated with the **leather** scene.

dental dam noun: a form of safer sex, where a piece of latex is fitted over the vagina or anus, usually used during oral sex.

dethroned adjective: forced to leave a public toilet.

diesel dike noun: a masculine lesbian.

dike, dyke noun: a **lesbian**, sometimes derogatory, although also reclaimed by some lesbians. In nineteenth century slang *dike* referred to male clothing and carried the connotation of masculine behaviour or appearance.

dike bite noun: the use of lesbianism as a feminist argument or as a way of insulting men.

dike daddy noun: a man who has lots of lesbians as friends. A younger male version of a dike daddy is a *dyke-tyke.*

dikes on spikes noun: lesbians who play softball.

dildo noun: a device shaped like a phallus which can be used for sexual stimulation. Many dildos are realistically created from latex in life-like colours with the outlines of veins on the surface, and some are made from a cast of a porn star's penis. See also **vibrator**.

dildo harness noun: a small harness, worn like underwear, which can hold a **dildo**, making it appear like an erect penis under clothing.

dildo training noun: to use a dildo, or series of different sized dildos in order to prepare the anus for penetration, or (in the case of males) as part of an emasculation roleplay.

dinge queen noun: a gay man who finds black men attractive.

DINK noun: acronym for *Dual Income No Kids,* referring to a gay or lesbian couple in a long-term relationship without children. DINKs, with their hypothesized large joint incomes and love of 'nest-building' are one of the favourite targets of **pink pound** advertising campaigns.

Dioning noun: a heterosexual male object of gay lust. Used in the 1860s by Karl Heinrich Ulrichs. See **Urning**.

direct action noun: a form of activism where participants are physically involved in trying to change a social or political order, via protest or demonstration. In the US ACT UP, Queer Nation and the Lesbian Avengers are direct action groups. In the UK the most well-known direct action group is OutRage. See also **zap action**.

dirty Sanchez noun: a form of **scat** play which involves smearing shit over a submissive partner's upper lip, leaving a kind of Mexican 'moustache'.

dis verb: to be abusive or disrespectful towards someone.

discipline noun: a form of erotic play involving training, punishing or correcting a partner. Often linked with **bondage**. See **BDSM**.

disco diva noun: 1. someone who loves clubbing and has very flamboyant, stylized dance moves. 2. a female pop singer e.g. Donna Summer, Kylie Minogue.

disco nap noun: a short period of sleep or rest, in order to prepare for a night of clubbing.

disco tits noun: pumped-up pectoral muscles that are displayed when a **gym queen** takes off his top on the dance floor.

discreet adjective: often used in personal adverts to imply that someone does not tell others about his/her sexual partners.

dish queen noun: a gay man who loves to gossip.

diva noun: a female singer who is popular among gay men. Divas often have tragic, complicated private lives or maintain a bitchy or haughty façade. Divas are divine. For example, Mae West, Judy Garland, Barbra Streisand, Liza Minelli, Bette Midler, Shirley Bassey. Elton John is an honorary diva. Divas are often referred to by their first name only: e.g. 'You've never heard of Barbra? Are you sure you're gay?' Gay men and divas can have a symbiotic, yet troubled relationship with one another – some divas may be ambivalent about legions of gay men worshipping them. See also **disco diva, female impersonator, gay icon**.

DL adjective: acronym for *Down Low* – black men who appear heterosexual in public, but have gay sex. US African-American slang.

docking verb: placing the foreskin of an uncircumcized penis over the head of another man's penis.

dogs in a bathtub noun: the act of trying to insert your testicles into the anus of someone who is being fucked.

doll house noun: a **drag queen** or **transvestite's** club, bar or meeting place. Also *TV lounge.*

dolly noun: a camp gay man who has become world-weary. UK slang.

dolly domestic noun: a gay man who has settled down into a long-term relationship.

dolphin noun: a piece of jewellery which joins two **Prince Alberts** together.

dom, dominant noun: a person who assumes sexual control (and possibly other forms of control) over a submissive partner.

domestic partnership noun: official recognition of partners (either homosexual or heterosexual) who are not legally married but cohabit and share a committed relationship.

dominatrix noun: a female **dom**. Also *domina, domme.*

don't ask, don't tell noun: a policy adopted in the US by Bill Clinton's government in 1993 to allow gays to serve in the military as long as they kept their sexuality a secret and didn't engage in gay sex.

don't be getting up in my world vocative: keep your nose out of my business. US. **drag queen** slang.

don't go there vocative: a warning for someone to change the subject or leave something alone. US.

dot noun: a quick peck on the cheek. UK. See also **dash**.

double bagger noun: someone who is so ugly that in order to have sex with him or her you'd need two bags – one for their head and the other for yours.

double ender noun: a **dildo** which can be used to penetrate two people simultaneously.

double feature noun: sex with one person and then with another immediately afterwards.

double penetration, DP noun: two penises entering an anus simultaneously.

double ribs noun: pertaining to male homosexuality. From ancient China.

drab noun: 1. the everyday clothing worn by your birth sex – the opposite of **drag**. 2. an acronym of *Dressed as a boy*.

drag noun: 1. clothing typical of one sex or gender worn by the opposite sex or gender. However, drag can often be much more than clothing, and reflects a mental, emotional or sexual state of being. Some transgendered people have pointed out that the real 'drag' is to have to wear the clothing that is socially expected of them. 2. any clothing not worn by the speaker in their everyday life. 'Have you seen David in all his butch uniform drag? I wonder where he'll put his handbag?' 3. an acronym of *Dressed as a girl*.

dragazine noun: a magazine for or about **drag queens**.

drag butch noun: a butch female who can pass for a heterosexual male.

drag diva noun: a breath-takingly attractive **drag queen** or **transvestite**.

drag hag noun: someone who likes the company of drag queens.

drag king noun: a lesbian who dresses as a man. Also *drag boy, faux man*.

drag princess noun: a young **drag queen**, especially one who is exceptionally effeminate or pretty.

drag queen noun: a gay man who dresses as a woman, and often flamboyantly exaggerates female mannerisms.

drag queen name noun: a person's drag queen name is said to be the name of their first pet coupled with the name of the first street they lived in (or their mother's maiden name). See also **camp name, porn star name**.

drag show noun: a performance at a gay bar or club featuring a **female impersonator** or **drag queen**.

drag sister noun: a friend of a **drag queen**, who also happens to be a drag queen.

drag slave noun: someone who assists a **drag queen** in getting ready for a show.

drag time noun: about one to two hours later than the actual time given. **Drag queen** slang, quoted in Darrin Hagen's *The Edmonton Queen* (1997). Sometimes referred to as *gay time*.

drama noun: a personal emotional turmoil or incident such as discovering your boyfriend in bed with your neighbour.

drama queen noun: anybody (but especially a gay man) whose emotional response tends to be exaggerated in every situation. 'Nigel's such a drama queen, his whole life is one long Oscar acceptance speech.'

drop a hairpin verb: to hint that one is gay.

dungeon noun: a space where **S&M** activity occurs, often furnished with specialist equipment. Dungeons can also occur in cyber-space.

dutch boy noun: men, either gay or straight, who like to have lesbians as friends. Also *honorary lesbian, male lesbian*.

dutch girl noun: lesbian. Derived from the term **dike**/ dyke.

dutch oven noun: 1. the act of farting in bed while pulling the sheets over one's head. 2. the act of farting into someone's mouth. Also *greek sauna.*

dykedar noun: the ability to tell that someone is a lesbian. Derived from **gaydar**.

dykon noun: a *lesbian icon,* specifically people or things who are admired by or representative of gay women e.g. k.d. lang, Ellen Degeneres, Jodie Foster.

E

E noun: Ecstasy, a synthetic, psychoactive drug with stimulant and hallucinogenic properties which is popular among clubbers. Its chemical structure: 3–4 methylene-dioxymethamphetamine gives it the acronym *MDMA* although it is also known as *Adam, hug beans, love drug, X* and *XTC*. Side effects can include confusion, depression, nausea, paranoia, faintness, blurred vision, chills or sweating, increase in heart rate and changes in the brain's level of dopamine and serotonin which can lead to long-term or permanent damage to parts of the brain critical for thought, memory and pleasure. See **X queen**.

ear muffs noun: small animals, usually dogs and cats who are suitable pets for apartments in cities.

earring code noun: in the 1970s and 1980s, wearing an earring or stud in the left ear was supposed to signify that you were gay. In the 1990s, some gay men changed the code, wearing an earring in both ears.

earthy-crunchy dyke noun: a New Age or Neo-Pagan

lesbian. Earthy-crunchy dykes are often vegetarian or vegan. Also *extra-crunchy*.

eating dead babies verb: to be caught with lipstick on your teeth. **Drag queen** slang, quoted in Darrin Hagen's *The Edmonton Queen* (1997).

edgeplay noun: one of the more controversial aspects of **S&M** roleplay, which focuses on activities that are on the 'edge' of safety. For example, **breath control, feeder**.

electroplay, electrotorture noun: the use of electrical devices during **S&M** roleplay for sexual stimulation.

emasculation noun: the feminization of males – in mainstream society this is often carried out negatively and as a way of asserting and maintaining existing power hierarchies – for example by referring to all gay men as sissies. However, there exists the concept of 'positive emasculation', cases where a man may set aside his masculinity, perhaps temporarily, for a number of reasons: as a cathartic exercise, to experience what it is like to be a woman, for sexual reasons, to make a **gender fuck** statement etc. See also **forced feminization**.

encourager noun: someone who wants to make his partner put on weight. **Chub** slang. See also **feeder**.

en drabbe adjective: the state of a **cross-dresser** when wearing the clothes of their birth sex. See also **drab, en femme**.

en femme adjective: the state of a **cross-dresser** who is wearing their preferred clothing.

enthroned adjective: to be in a public toilet and looking for sex. See **dethroned**.

eonism noun: transvestitism, coined by Havelock Ellis to describe the famous French cross-dresser Chevalier d'Eon.

essentialism noun: the theory that homosexuals are born and that sexuality is therefore biologically determined. This view was supported when the existence of a so-called **gay gene** was discovered, which was passed down by the mother. See also **social constructionism**.

ethical slut noun: popularized by Dozzie Easton and Catherine A. Liszt, in their book *The Ethical Slut: A Guide To Infinite Sexual Possibilities* (1997) an *ethical slut* is one who participates in honest and consensual, open or multiple partner relationships. Easton and Liszt's philosophy is 'sex is nice and pleasure is good for you'.

etre aux hommes adjective: to be gay. From French Candian. Also *homme aux homes, moumoune.*

evil adjective: describes a variety of feelings, from that which you only mildly dislike or are ambivalent about, to that which is truly hateful. 'Sweetie, why are you wearing that t-shirt! It's evil!'

ex-gay noun: someone who claims to have once been homosexual but isn't any more. Ex-gays are often involved in religious communities.

extravadraganza noun: a film which features drag queens, cross-dressing or transvestitism in a positive light. For example, *The Adventures of Priscilla Queen of the Desert* (1994), *The Iron Ladies* (2000).

extreme watersports noun: taking a sexual fetish for urine to an extreme level: for example, by going into a men's room in a club and licking the urinals and floor. See also **watersports**.

eye candy noun: an attractive person.

F

FA noun: acronym for *Fat Admirers*. See **chub**.

fab pad noun: a great apartment.

fabulous adjective: good. Also *fabu, faboo*.

facial noun: the experience of having one (or more) males ejaculating onto the face. See **bukkake**.

factory equipped noun: a biological male (as opposed to a **f-t-m transsexual**). Also *bio boy, gen man*.

fag, faggot noun: 1. gay man, usually derogatory. Leigh Rutledge (1996) in *The New Gay Book of Lists* suggests five possible origins. i) Since the fourteenth century, a bundle of sticks or twigs tied together for use as fuel was called a *faggot*. The word was specifically used with reference to the practice of burning heretics or 'sodomites' alive at the stake. ii) As far back as the 1500s disagreeable women were referred to as *faggots*. It is possible that this slang term may have been widened to refer to homosexuals at some point. iii) In nineteenth century British public schoolboy slang, to *fag* was to perform duties for older boys such as polishing boots, running errands, warming a cold toilet seat for them. This system contained some sexual overtones. iv) In World War I cigarettes were referred to in British slang as *fags* and were regarded by some as unmanly in comparison to pipes or cigars. v) Judy Grahn in her book *Another Mother Tongue* (1990) writes that the faggot was a wand for divination and sacred firemaking and has belonged to the province of gay male wizards, sorcerers and priests for thousands of years. 2. an acronym of *Factory Accessorized Gay* meaning a **f-t-m transsexual** who is also gay.

fag drag noun: a **drag king** who sometimes performs a gay male identity.

fag hag noun: the female friend of a gay man. See **fruit fly**.

fag mag noun: a magazine or other publication geared towards gay men or lesbians.

fag magnet noun: any event which draws a large gay or lesbian audience.

fag stag noun: a heterosexual man who chooses to socialize with groups of gay men.

fairy noun: twentieth century pejorative slang for an effeminate gay man. Also *belle, bunny, buttercup, daffodil, daisy, flit, flossy, fluff, fruit, fruitcake, lavender boy, lily, Mary, nance, nancyboy, nelly, pansy, poof, poove, powder-puff, puff, sissie, swish. Fairy* was **reclaim**ed in the late twentieth century as *radical faerie,* to denote gay men who refuse to take traditional masculine roles. Can also be used to refer to femme transvestites who wear fairy-like clothing.

fairy godmother noun: 1. a mythical role model alluded to by **drag queens**. 2. an older, experienced drag queen.

family noun: the gay and lesbian community. A number of words that are used to describe gay men are taken from family relationships: **sister** (Polari entry), **daddy**, **son**, *mother*, **auntie** (Polari entry), **grandma**. 'Is he family?'

fatherfelcher noun: a male equivalent to *motherfucker*.

feeder noun: a dominant partner in **D&S** who takes pleasure in watching their partner consume large amounts of food. Feeding may be considered to be long-term **edge-play** in that obesity can cause serious health problems. See also **FA**.

feigele, feygele adjective: Yiddish expression meaning to be gay, from the word for 'bird'.

felch verb: 1. an extremely rare (to the extent of being apocryphal) sexual practice involving placing a live animal (usually a small rodent or fish) into someone's anus. Dangerous and cruel to animals. See also **gerbil jamming**. 2. to suck semen from someone's anus after anal sex.

fem, femme 1. noun: a gay man or lesbian who acts and dresses in a feminine manner. 2. adjective: to be feminine in behaviour or dress. See **high femme, low femme**.

female faggot noun: a woman who passes as a man, and also has 'gay' relationships with men. See **transfag**.

female female impersonator noun: a woman (usually an entertainer) who gives an exaggeratedly feminine performance e.g. Mae West, Jayne Mansfield, Marilyn Monroe.

female guiche noun: a female perineal piercing. See **guiche**.

female impersonator noun: a cabaret performer (usually a gay male) who dresses as a woman, usually a **gay icon** or **diva** and dances, sings or mimes in front of an audience.

female symbol noun: a circle with a line descending from its lowermost part, and intersected at the end. Two female symbols linked together represent lesbian sexuality. See also **male symbol**.

fem fatale noun: an effeminate gay man.

femme finishing school noun: a place where **m-t-f transsexuals, drag queens** and **transvestites** can learn feminine behaviour and abilities.

fierce adjective: sassy, hot, fashionable. A compliment when paid to a **drag queen**.

fifth wheel noun: a heterosexual person in a group of gay people.

fifty-fifty verb: to alternate between oral and anal sex.

final girl noun: a woman in a slasher or horror film who is the only survivor when all of her friends have been killed by a monster or stalker e.g. the character played by Jamie Lee Curtis in *Halloween* or Sigourney Weaver in the *Alien* series. The final girl is usually slightly butch and/or hasn't had sex with any of the men in the film (and is therefore said to represent the belief that 'real' men don't want unfeminine women). Any woman who is slightly butch or androgynous can be therefore referred to as a *final girl*.

fine adjective: attractive. Also *foyne*.

finger, finger fuck verb: to insert one or more fingers into the anus or vagina. The term can also be used to refer to a rectal examination by a doctor (especially one who's attractive).

finocchio noun: a gay man, often used to denote effeminacy. Derived from Italian slang and referring to the fennel plant.

Fire Island noun: a barrier island off the coast of Long Island, New York, which is famous for two gay beach resorts: **Cherry Grove** and Fire Island **Pines**.

fire queen noun: a gay man who likes to burn other men for sexual gratification.

fish and chips noun: the wife and children of a man who has gay sex. UK.

fish queen noun: a person (usually heterosexual male) who likes to perform cunnilingus.

fishwife noun: a woman who is married to a gay man.

fist, fistfuck, FF verb: the extreme sexual practice of inserting the hand into the anus or vagina. See also **handballing, spleening**.

flagging verb: to use colour-coded bandanas or handkerchiefs (or keys) in order to signify one's sexual preferences or kinks. See **hanky code, key code**.

flamer, flaming queen noun: an outrageous, flamboyantly camp, gay man.

flannel shirt dyke noun: a capable, 'outdoorsy' lesbian.

flavour noun: gender expression. US. African-American gay slang.

flick off verb: to masturbate (women).

flip verb: 1. to turn a **top** into a **bottom**. 2. to make a **stone butch** 'allow' herself to be touched either physically or emotionally.

flip-flop noun: 1. a bisexual person. 2. someone who can be femme or butch. 3. sex between two men where both partners take turns at getting fucked.

floss verb: to get pubic hair caught in the teeth when performing oral sex or rimming.

fluffer noun: someone who is employed to facilitate a male porn actor's erection (usually via oral stimulation), just before his performance. Entered gay slang via films such as *Hustler White* (1996) and *The Fluffer* (2001).

fluffy 1. noun: a woman who is sexually aroused. Lesbian slang. 2. adjective: someone who isn't into a particular dress code, e.g. the leather scene. Derived from descriptions of people who wear big fluffy sweaters.

FNG noun acronym for *Fucking New Guy* (from 1960s Vietnam War slang to describe a newly assigned soldier who was considered likely to get himself and experienced soldiers killed). Used to refer to a **f-t-m transsexual** who joins a support group and immediately starts to assert his opinions and take charge.

foot-play noun: erotic interactions with feet. See also **shrimping**.

foot worship noun: a form of **body worship** which involves sucking, kissing and licking the bare feet. Also known as *foot service*. A *foot queen* is a gay man who is into foot worship.

forced feminization noun: a form of **D&S** roleplay where a female or transvestite **top** 'forces' a male **bottom** to wear female underwear and other clothing. The bottom will have either consented in advance to the roleplay, or have requested it. In some cases the bottom will be penetrated with a dildo, or fucked by another man, while the top watches and verbally controls the situation.

foreskin restoration noun: the act of recreating a foreskin on a **cut** penis by stretching and other means.

foursome, fourway, forgy noun: sex between four people.

fox noun: a predatory, older gay man, particularly one who likes **chickens** (see Polari entry).

fragrance fairy noun: a camp gay man who is employed to spray samples of aftershave at passing customers in a large department store.

freak dance verb: to dance while rubbing your genital area over another person's body.

freedom rings noun: a necklace comprised of aluminium rings in the colours of the **rainbow flag**. Can also be made into earrings, rings and bracelets. Sometimes triangles are substituted for rings. Also known as **fruit loops**.

french noun: oral sex, derived from 1960s personal advertising slang. *French Active* or *FRA* is to give oral sex, while *French Passive* or *FRP* is to receive it.

French embassy noun: any place where gay sex is easily available, especially a gym or YMCA.

French maid noun: fantasy roleplay where a male or female bottom dresses as a 'french maid' and serves food etc. The uniform usually consists of a short dress, frilly petticoat, frilly apron, stockings, high-heels, lacy headpiece, lace wrist-cuffs and white gloves.

frenum ladder noun: a series of piercings forming a ladder up the shaft of the penis.

fresh meat noun: a new person (usually young and/or attractive) on the gay scene.

friend of Dorothy noun: a gay man. Originates from the fact that a lot of gay men have been fans of Judy Garland who played Dorothy in the film *The Wizard of Oz* (1939). The birth of Gay Liberation is linked to the police raid of the Stonewall Inn, a New York gay bar on the night of Friday, 27 June 1969. The patrons were already at a low point following the death of Judy Garland on 22 June and this was the last straw – they decided to fight back.

frig verb: 1. masturbation. 2. mutual masturbation between two women.

frighten the horses verb: to cause shock or dismay because of your sexuality or gender behaviour, especially when witnessed by so-called 'normal' people. Also *frighten the mundanes, freak the mundanes*.

frock noun: a man who is romantically paired with a lesbian in order to keep her sexuality a secret: the male equivalent of a **beard**.

frock star noun: a male rock or pop star who wears female clothing either privately, or as part of his act.

frog queen noun: 1. a gay man who is attracted to French men. 2. a French-Canadian gay man. Derogatory.

front marriage noun: a marriage of convenience between a lesbian and gay man, for the sake of society, work or the family.

frottage noun: a form of non-penetrative sex involving rubbing parts of the body (usually the genitals) against someone.

frottage queen noun: someone who derives pleasure from **frottage**. 'John had sticky pants again after he hooked up with another frottage queen on the subway.'

fruit fly noun: a term for heterosexual women who like to socialize with gay men and **drag queens**. Also **fag hag**, *flame dame, gay goddess, princess with a pink wand, ribbon clerk.*

fruit loops noun: 1. **freedom rings**. 2. a gay cruising area. 'Jack's spent all night out on the fruit loop again.'

fruit picker noun: a mostly heterosexual man who will occasionally take gay male partners.

f-t-m, ftm, F2M adjective: acronym for *female to male,* referring to a woman who either wants to **cross-dress** as, or become, a man. Also *aftermarket, recast male, TMan, transman.*

FTV noun: a female **transvestite**.

FUBAR vocative: acronym for *Fucking U Beyond All Recognition.* Internet chatroom slang.

fuck verb: to have sex, usually to penetrate the vagina or anus with a penis (or similarly shaped object). Also *ball,* *bang, boff, bonk, boop, dick, do, do a bit of rough, flap skin, get one's flue cleaned, get one's rocks off, go all the way, hide the salami/sausage/weenie, hump, jump on someone's bones, legover, make it, mount, party, plough, poke, pork, pound, prod, pump, ride, roger, score, screw, scrump, sew wild oats, shag, slam, stab, work.*

fuck boy noun: a submissive male adult sex partner. Also *fuck girl, fuck slave, fuck toy.*

fuck buddy, FB noun: a regular casual sex partner, where there is little or no emotional involvement.

fuck date noun: a date where both parties know that the only reason for meeting each other is to have sex.

fuck flat noun: an apartment or house where sex often takes place. 'Please tell me you didn't go back to Colin's little fuck flat!'

fuck me raw vocative: indicates surprise or shock.

fuck of death noun: becoming infected with **HIV** during sex. From **barebacking** slang.

full house noun: having more than one sexually transmitted disease at the same time.

full time/part time adjective: the extent to which a **cross-dresser** lives in his or her desired gender role.

G

gaff noun: a device used by **cross-dressing** males in order to hide the bulge of their penis. See **tuck**.

GAGA adjective: acronym for *Gay Acting, Gay Appearing*. See **SASA**.

gag reflex noun: it was believed that gay men had no 'gag reflex' because they were used to performing fellatio. This was used as a test by army doctors in World War II. In order to determine if a soldier was homosexual a tongue depressor was inserted into the man's throat to see if he gagged.

gainer noun: someone who either gains weight or wants to put on weight because he or she finds it sexually appealing. **Chub** slang.

galimony, gayimony noun: the lesbian and gay versions of palimony, where one partner claims part of another's earnings after a split.

GAM adjective: personal advertising acronym for *Gay Asian Male*. A Gay Asian Female is *GAF*.

gang bang noun: 1. group sex. Also *cluster fuck, group grope, orgy, pricknic*. See **horrorgy**. 2. the rape of one (or more) participants by a group.

gardening verb: cruising in open spaces, e.g. a park or area of woodland near a public toilet. UK. Someone who does this is a *bush queen*.

gas leak verb: to attempt to silently break wind while receiving oral sex.

gauging verb: the act of stretching a pierced part of the body.

gay adjective/noun: homosexual. *Gay* has an illustrious etymology, with one of its earliest meanings being 'disposed to joy and mirth', or of a horse 'lively, prancing.' In the seventeenth century, a *gay dog* was a man given to revelling or self-indulgence. Poetry was called the 'gay science' in the early nineteenth century, and when first used on women it was as an epithet or as praise. In the nineteenth century *gay* had come to mean an immoral woman who lived a life of prostitution. By the late nineteenth century in the US it had come to mean someone who was over-familiar or impertinent. A *gay tail* was an erect dog's tail. By the early twentieth century *gay* was applied to homosexuality, although in 1950's UK it was mostly only used by 'upmarket queens'. By the early 1970s the Gay Liberation Front helped to publicize *gay* as a word with positive connotations. More recently, the word has been used by teenagers to refer to something as being lame or unfashionable. Also *Auntie Em, bender, blade, bum boy, cakeboy,* **cock sucker**, *confirmed bachelor,* **fag**, **family**, *flamer,* **friend of Dorothy**, *fruit, gander, ginger, goes to our church, happy, jessie, jolly, left handed, light on his loafers, minty, moxy, one of us, on the other bus, on the program, queer, same-sex oriented, sings in the choir, so, sugar in his pants*. See **active**, **fairy**, **passive**.

gay brain noun: a theory published in the journal *Science* in 1991 by Dr Simon LeVay who found that a tiny section of the hypothalamus in the brain was smaller in gay men than in straight men. In 1992 Allen and Gorski found that a section of the fibres connecting the right and left hemispheres of the brain is one-third larger in gay men than straight men (*Proceedings of the National Academy of Sciences of the USA*). See also **gay gene**.

gay card noun: a mythological 'card' which allows the owner access into the gay community. Some nightclubs with strict 'gay only' policies will only let suspect non-gays in unless they can play a gay card, for example, by naming several other gay clubs in the area or by kissing a person of the same sex.

gaydar noun: the ability to pick up on (sometimes extremely subtle) clues which allow a person to recognize gay men and lesbians. In general, the more time spent in gay and lesbian company, the more enhanced a person's gaydar will be. Gay men and lesbians often have better gaydar anyway because of the *interested eye phenomenon* – the ability to perceive things that interest the observer, even though other people are trying to be discreet.

gaydom noun: the 'world' of gay men and lesbians; not a real place, but includes everyone who ever lived who was gay and everything associated with homosexuality.

gay for pay adjective: a heterosexual who works as a gay male prostitute or a gay porn star who claims to be 'just doing it for the money'.

gay friendly adjective: referring to a business or place which accepts gay lifestyles and welcomes gay people.

gay gene noun: the theory that homosexuality can be passed down via DNA. Studies carried out in the early–mid 1990s claimed to pinpoint a specific genetic marker on the X chromosome linked to male homosexuality. For example, Dean Hamer published research in *Science* 261 (1993) which found that in 40 pairs of gay brothers, 33 had the same set of DNA sequences in a region of the Xq28 chromosome. His follow-up study in 1995 had similar findings. However, a more recent study by George Rice *et al.* in *Science* 284 (1999) which looked at 52 pairs of gay brothers found that their Xq28 sequences were no more similar than what would be expected via chance. It may be the case that the gay gene exists elsewhere, or that many genes are involved in homosexuality, or that other factors (for example, society or upbringing) are more important. See also **essentialism, gay brain**.

gay ghetto noun: a derogatory term for any geographical space where significantly large numbers of gay men and lesbians live, work or enjoy leisure activities. This term would be most likely used by people who believe that gay and straight communities should be more integrated.

gay icon noun: 1. any person or thing who represents an aspect or aesthetic of homosexuality in some way e.g. Quentin Crisp, RuPaul, the **rainbow flag**. 2. an object of gay male lust e.g. Robbie Williams, Ricky Martin, Matt Dillon. 3. a **diva** or other famous woman such as Bette Davis, Joan Crawford or more recently Patsy and Edina from *Absolutely Fabulous* who are worshipped for being excessive, stylish, melodramatic, camp, strong and bitchy. See **dykon**.

Gayle noun: a gay language variety used in South Africa, originating among black gay men in the 1950s and used in the 1970s and 1980s in white gay communities in Johannesburg, Cape Town and Durban, spread by white airline stewards. While Gayle contains many terms from **Polari** and US based gay slang, it also includes an impressive vocabulary of words based on alliteration with women's names. See also **Abigail, Barbara Iris, koffiemoffie, Lettie, Mona, Nora, Pandora, Rita, Vera**.

gay lib, gay liberation noun: see **GLF**.

gay mafia noun: a covert and powerful group of gay men and/or lesbians. Also *lavender mafia, pink mafia*. See also **A-Gay, power lesbian**.

gay sauna noun: a UK **bath-house**, usually having a Swedish sauna cabin, steam-room, Jacuzzi, video-room, rest areas, showers, and bar/café. Also *health-club*.

gay spray noun: an imaginary 'spray' used when gay men decorate a new home, in order to make it more amenable to their tastes (*Will and Grace*).

gay village noun: an informal name for an urban area in a city which contains a proportionally large number of gay-run, gay-owned or gay-friendly businesses or dwellings. In the UK this would refer to Old Compton Street in London's Soho and Canal Street in Manchester. See also **gay ghetto**.

gay widower noun: a heterosexual man who is in a relationship with a **fag-hag**, or **drag-hag** and is left home alone while she parties with her gay or transgendered friends.

gazoopy verb: to perform sexually for money.

GBF noun: acronym for *Gay Black Female.*

GBM noun: acronym for *Gay Black Male.*

gender noun: *gender* can be a troubling term to identify, as its meanings differ depending on whom is giving the definition. For example, Humm in *The Dictionary of Feminist Theory* (1989: 84) refers to gender as a 'culturally-shaped group of attributes and behaviours given to the female or to the male.' Jennifer Coates in *Women, Men and Language* (1993: 4) agrees, taking sex to refer to the biological distinction between men and women, whereas gender describes socially constructed categories based on sex. Eve Sedgwick in *Epistemology of the Closet* (1991: 27) describes gender as the 'dichotomized social production of male and female identities and behaviours – of male and female persons – in a cultural system for which "male/female" functions as a primary and perhaps model binarism . . .'. Judith Butler in *Gender Trouble: Feminism and the Subversion of Identity* (1990) related this idea to gendered identities, suggesting that their presentation is a never-ending process:

> Gender is the repeated stylization of the body, a set of repeated acts within a highly rigid regulatory frame that congeal over time to produce the appearance of substance of a natural sort of being.
>
> (Butler 1990: 33)

This conceptualization of gender extends earlier feminist theory (e.g. Simone de Beauvoir) that one is not born but becomes a woman. According to Butler (1990: 33), becoming a woman is 'a term in process, a beginning, a constructing that cannot rightfully be said to originate or to end'.

In the strategy of naming sex as 'the act, and only the act', Kate Bornstein, a transgendered person, attempts to remove biology from the arena of gender definition in *My Gender Workbook* (1998: 26). She radically refers to gender as any form of categorization, 'whether it's appearance or mannerisms, biology or psychology, hormones, roles, genitals . . .', whereas sex is 'fucking: any way, shape or form, alone or with another or others'.

The act of defining gender is laid open to further confusion when one considers the terms 'masculine' and 'feminine', and what they are supposed to mean, both in terms of how they relate to one another and how we are supposed to measure them. Some theorists have attempted to understand gender by basing it around metaphorical constructs. For Coates (1993: 4) gender can be thought of in terms of a continuum or continua, in that some men (or women) may be more masculine or feminine than others. Bornstein (1998: 42–5) prefers to think of gender as a pyramid of power, with the most 'perfectly gendered' people (white, male, American, middle-aged, rich, heterosexual etc.) at the top and 'less perfectly' gendered people existing further down. Certainly a model or metaphor of gender would have to take into account the fact that gender is not a static category, changing for each person over time. It is also extremely subjective, being a personal experience based in part upon the mores of any given society, and it cannot be defined on the basis of any one behaviour, but is the interaction of a complex and changing set of internal and external thoughts and behaviours, which are also connected to both biology and sexuality.

gender bender noun: a person who pushes the boundaries of accepted gender, sex or sexuality norms (especially a pop singer) e.g. Boy George. Originally derogatory 1980's UK tabloid slang. The term *gender benderella,* coined in the US in the 1990s has been used to refer to people like *Saturday Night Live*'s 'Pat' or k.d. lang. On the other hand a *bender* is derogatory slang for a homosexual – perhaps linked to the fact that gay men are supposed to bend over in order to be penetrated anally, or associated with the word *bent* – early twentieth century slang for homosexual.

gender butcher noun: someone who attempts to alter their gender, but does so in an unattractive way.

gender fuck noun: anything that emulates aspects of the opposite sex, usually to shock others or make them question assumptions. For example: a man wearing strap-on breasts under his suit or a woman who has a strap-on dildo in her jeans. Gender fuck can be construed as political in that it challenges traditional notions of 'accepted' behaviour.

gender girl noun: a biological female, one born with a vagina, as opposed to a **drag queen, a transsexual** or

transvestite. Also called *genetic girl, GG, genetic woman genwoman, GW, real girl.*

gender identity noun: how a person perceives their **gender**.

gender identity disorder noun: a medical term used to denote someone who strongly identifies with the opposite sex. Also *gender dysphoria, GID.*

gender reassignment surgery noun: the surgery required to change a person's sex. Also *go to Denmark, GRS, sex-change.*

gentleman butch noun: a masculine lesbian who has good manners.

gerbil jamming verb: a form of **felching** which involves putting a gerbil or other small rodent inside a condom, which is then placed inside a lubricated paper towel roll that is inserted into the rectum. The paper towel roll is yanked out, leaving the bagged gerbil inside, where it will suffocate and die. This apocryphal practice is obviously dangerous and cruel to animals.

get her vocative: who does he think he is?

get over it vocative: you need to move on and stop obsessing about this.

get over yourself vocative: don't be so self-centred.

GHM adjective: personal advertising acronym for *Gay Hispanic Male.* A Gay Hispanic Female is *GHF.*

GIB adjective: acronym for *Good In Bed.*

gift (the) noun: a sexually transmitted disease, usually **HIV** . **Barebacking** slang.

gift-givers noun: men who are **HIV** positive and are willing to infect **bug chasers**. **Barebacking** slang.

gillette blade noun: a bisexual woman.

gimp noun: a submissive participant in **BDSM** sex. Also *gimp mask, gimp suit* – clothing usually made of tight-fitting, black rubber or leather. 'Bring out the gimp!' *Pulp Fiction* (1994).

girl noun: 1. a general gay term of address, to be used on anyone. 2. a **bottom** in **BDSM** who is femme and roleplays as young.

girlfriend noun: 1. a gay male friend, not a sexual partner. From African-American and **drag queen** slang. 2. a lesbian's lover.

glam adjective: glamorous.

glamazon noun: a **drag queen**. US.

glamour butch noun: a butch lesbian who likes to wear suits or tuxedos.

glass closet noun: the delusion that a person is in the closet, when in fact their sexuality is obvious to everyone. 'Harry thinks he's so straight-acting, but he's just living in a big glass closet!'

GLB noun: acronym for *Gay, Lesbian and Bisexual*. Also *LGB*.

GLBT noun: acronym for *Gay, Lesbian Bisexual and Transgendered*. Also written as *LGBT*.

GLF noun: acronym for *Gay Liberation Front*. The Stonewall Inn riot of 1969 united gay bar culture and gay activists, resulting in the gay liberation movement, which was particularly popular from 1969 to 1973. Gay Liberationists rejected the idea of social assimilation and were more confrontational than groups such as the UK-based Campaign For Homosexual Equality (**CHE**) and the US-based **Mattachine Society**. Gay Liberation was also a struggle against sexism, a common belief being that roles such as butch and femme were ultimately restricting. In the UK many of GLF members had previously been in groups that had been influenced by Marxist politics and they brought with them an emphasis on counterculture, individualism and a dislike of hierarchies and capitalism. The GLF carried out a form of **zap action** against the Festival of Light, of which the 'clean-up television' campaigner Mary Whitehouse was a chief co-ordinator. They released mice into the audience, dressed as nuns, heckled speakers and unfolded a giant banner proclaiming singer Cliff Richard as the Queen of England.

glut noun: someone with an appetite for performing fellatio that can never be satisfied.

go commando verb: to not wear underwear.

go down verb: to perform oral sex on someone.

go girl vocative: supportive and encouraging phrase meaning 'you're doing well'. From **drag queen** slang.

gogo boy noun: a young, attractive man who is paid to dance on a podium in a nightclub, wearing a jockstrap.

golden shower noun: the act of urinating on someone, for sexual gratification. Also known as *GS* and *pissplay*. See **watersports**.

gold star lesbian noun: a lesbian who has never had sex with a man and never intends to.

government-inspected meat noun: gay men in the armed forces.

Grand Canyon noun: a very slack anus.

grande adjective: aloof, haughty or pretentious.

grandma, granny noun: an old gay man. 'Don't bother going in the steam-room, it's full of grandmas.' UK.

granola lesbian noun: a health-conscious lesbian. See **earthy-crunchy dyke**.

grazing verb: **soaking**, while walking along. UK slang.

greek noun: anal intercourse. Used in 1960s personal advertising slang. *Greek Active* (to **top**) is *GRA* while *Greek Passive* (to **bottom**) is *GRP*.

green queen noun: a gay man who likes to have sex outdoors, particularly in parks or areas of woodland.

grizzly bear noun: an extremely hairy, husky, muscular **bear**.

ground rules noun: a list of rules between two or more people setting out the boundaries of a relationship, especially relating to sex, **group** sex or **BDSM** sex. 'Bill and me have some ground rules when we have a three-some – we always have safe sex, we make sure nobody gets left out and we don't get emotionally involved with the third person.'

group noun: sex between more than two people. Sex with three people is usually referred to as a **threesome** (UK) or **threeway** (US).

group hug! vocative: a homage to 1980s sitcom *The Golden Girls*, where many episodes featured three or four of the main characters all hugging each other at once.

grower not a shower noun: a person who does not appear attractive or interesting upon first impressions, but over time his or her natural gifts shine through.

grr vocative: 1. a sign of affection. 2. leave me alone. **Bear** slang.

grrl noun: a young lesbian with **attitude**.

grrl code noun: a classificatory system, derived from the **bear code**, used to describe **grrls**. Various qualities receive ratings from !, !! or !!! (the extent to which the grrl possesses the trait) to *, **, or *** (the extent to which she doesn't possess the trait). For example: BL: Bi-les factor, the extent to which a grrl is a lesbian. !!! means totally lesbian. *** means heterosexual. Other traits include PA: political action factor, SF: silk/flannel factor (so !!! = wears trendy 'silk' clothing, *** = flannel clothing only). TP: tattoos and piercings. F: furriness (body hair). B/F: butch/femme. A: androgyny. V: vices. B: body (muscularity vs chub). G: 'go' factor (active vs sleepy). O: 'out' factor (openly lesbian vs in the closet). S: 'scream' factor (amount of noise made during sex). N: 'nesting' or commitment factor. K: kinkiness. H: head-case or mental instability. D/S: 'dom/sub' factor. TF: 'touchy-feely' factor. R: 'romance' factor. C: 'cultured' factor.

GSO noun: acronym for *Gay Significant Other.*

GSOH adjective: personal advert acronym for *Good Sense of Humour.*

guest star noun: the third person who makes up a **threesome** with a couple who are already in a relationship. 'I just love being the guest star, I get all the attention.'

guiche noun: a piercing behind the scrotum but in front of the anus.

guppies noun: acronym for *Gay Urban Professionals.* Derived from yuppie: *Young Urban Professional.* See **luppies**.

GWF adjective: personal advert acronym for *Gay White Female.*

GWM adjective: personal advert acronym for *Gay White Male.*

gymbot noun: a gay man whose entire life revolves around going to the gym – a gym robot.

gym bunny noun: a **gym queen** who is also effeminate.

gym queen noun: a gay man who spends lots of time working on muscle development. Also *Muscle Mary.*

gym tits noun: over-developed pectoral muscles as a result of working out at the gym.

gynaeotrope noun: a lesbian. Created by Kurt Hiller. See also **androtrope**.

H

HAART noun: acronym for *Highly Active Antiretroviral Therapy*. The use of a combination or cocktail of drugs to treat **HIV**.

hag noun: 1. an unpleasant or unattractive gay man. 2. an unattractive woman. Also *plain Jane*. See **hagism**.

hag-fag noun: a gay man who likes to hang out with lots of women. Derived from the more commonly used **fag-hag**.

hagism noun: a person's identification with a particular group (usually one which is united in terms of a shared sex, gender or sexuality) which they are not 'officially' a member of. For example, a heterosexual woman who likes gay men is a **fag-hag**. Hagism is sometimes seen as a psychological issue – the desire for a person to have what they cannot possess, or to live vicariously through the experiences of another. However, hags are generally viewed as liberal and fiercely supportive of the group they desire to associate with. See **fag-hag, drag-hag, hag-fag, spag-fag, stag-hag**.

hair burner noun: a gay beautician or hairdresser.

hair fairy noun: a gay man who is obsessed with his hair.

hand-balling verb: placing the hand into the anus or vagina. Some tops will 'ball' their hands into fists. See also **fisting, spleening**.

hand-job noun: to masturbate someone else to orgasm.

hanky code noun: coloured bandanas or handkerchiefs can be worn in order to signify or **flag** specific sexual interests or fetishes. The hanky code was originally conceived as a humorous article in *The Village Voice* in the 1970s which suggested that the gay men in New York would have an easier time making contacts if they used a more sophisticated system to the existing **key code**. The article suggested buying Levi bandanas from a local surplus store and suggested meanings of a few colours – red, navy, light blue, green and black. Although the article wasn't expected to be taken seriously, the gay community took it to heart. Dominants or tops will wear the bandana on the left side of their body (typically sticking out of a pocket), while bottoms or submissives will use the right side. This right/left flagging also applies to other forms of **BDSM** role play, so a dominant would wear a whip on the left side while a submissive who wanted to be whipped would wear it on the right. Some hanky colours and their meanings are listed in the table below:

COLOUR	WORN ON THE LEFT	WORN ON THE RIGHT
apricot	chub	chubby chaser
beige	rimmer	likes to be rimmed
black	extreme top	extreme bottom
black velvet	voyeur	exhibitionist
brown	top for watersports, scat and enemas	bottom for watersports, scat and enemas
charcoal	top with a latex/ rubber fetish	bottom with a latex/ rubber fetish

dark pink	likes to give tit torture	likes to receive tit torture
gold	two looking for a third	one looking for two
gray	likes bondage as a top	likes bondage as a bottom
houndstooth	likes to bite	likes to be bitten
kelly green	hustler	john
lavender	likes to top cross-dressers	likes to cross-dress
light blue	likes to be sucked	likes to suck cock
light pink	uses dildoes on people	likes to have dildoes used on them
navy blue	fucks	wants to get fucked
purple	likes to pierce	likes to be pierced
rust	likes to play with ponies	likes to 'be' a pony
tan	likes to smoke cigars and play with hot ash	wants to worship cigar smokers and receive hot ash
yellow	top, specifically for watersports	bottom for waterports

happy hips noun: a gay man who swishes his hips from side to side as he walks.

hard-off noun: to be sexually repulsed or turned off.

hard-on noun: 1. an erect penis. Also *apology, bar, big Jim and the twins, bone, boner, bowsprit, erection, flag pole, get it up, get wood, horn on, morning glory, piss hard, pudgy, rigid digit, rod, spike, staff, stiffie, stonker, throbber, woody.* 2. to like something: 'I've got such a hard-on for chocolate gateaux.'

hard up adjective: desperation due to a lack of sexual activity. 'I'm so hard up I'd fuck a whale's blowhole if the opportunity presented itself!'

harness noun: an item of fetish clothing, usually made of connected straps of leather embedded with metal studs.

having church verb: to kneel down in order to perform oral sex on someone. See **church**.

hazmat noun: the sexual fetishization of protective clothing (*haz*ardous *mat*erials) such as those worn by firefighters.

Hazzard country adjective: backwards or unfashionable. A reference to the early 1980s US television series *The Dukes of Hazzard*.

head play noun: any kind of manipulation by a **top** in order to heighten fear and anticipation in a **bottom** during **BDSM** roleplay. Also known as *head game, head trip, mind play, mind game*. See also **verbal abuse** and **mind fuck**.

head queen noun: a gay man who likes to give **blow jobs**.

helicoptering verb: the act of whacking an erect penis across someone's face during a strip-tease. See **tea-bag**.

helium heels noun: a man who likes to get fucked – so-called because his legs rise in the air.

hello vocative: A mixture of early 1990s Valley girl/drag queen slang, *hello* can be much more than a greeting. Used in a questioning tone (stress on the final syllable) 'I'm like, hel-*lo*?' the word can convey disbelief or impatience or function as an attention-getting device. It can also be used as an exclamation (stress mainly on the first syllable) '*Hel*-lo!' allowing the user to show surprise.

hell-sparking the pronoun verb: to use gender pronouns in a non-traditional way, either to cause confusion or to provoke thought. For example, using a generic 'she' rather than a generic 'he' in a magazine article. See also **gender game**.

herbals noun: over the counter herbal hormones which claim to be able to stimulate male or female hormones.

hermaphrodite noun: a person possessing both male and female sexual organs. Also *chick-with-dick, she-male.*

heterophobia noun: the hatred and fear of heterosexuality. One of the funniest heterophobes is the character of Aunt Ida played by Edith Massey in the John Waters film *Female Trouble* (1975). Aunt Ida tells her straight nephew Gator 'I worry that you'll get married, have children, work in an office. The world of the heterosexual is a sick and boring life.'

heterosexism noun: 1. the belief that heterosexuals are superior to bisexuals or homosexuals. 2. the assumption that everyone is heterosexual.

heterosexual privilege noun: a term used to describe how heterosexual co-workers are free to place photographs of loved ones on their desks, bring partners to work social events, and talk about their weekend activities and holidays without having to present an edited version of events, or be afraid of homophobic repercussions.

hettie, het noun: a slightly derogatory shortening of *heterosexual*. UK. See also **breeder**.

hide the candy verb: for a **drag queen** to conceal the bulge in the crotch with a **gaff**.

high drag noun: drag consisting of a beaded gown, a tiara and piled-on hair. **Drag queen** slang, from Darrin Hagen's *The Edmonton Queen* (1997). *Low drag* is anything else.

high femme noun: someone who is extremely feminine. See **low femme**.

hirsute noun: hairy, rough, shaggy, bristly (particularly of the body). From the Latin *hirsutus* and French *hirsute*. Used in gay advertising slang, and **bear** slang. It is most likely a coincidence that the word can also be pronounced as 'hair suit'.

HIV noun: acronym for *Human Immunodeficiency Virus*, which most people believe to be the major cause of **AIDS**. To be *HIV+* is to test positive for HIV antibodies, meaning that the virus is present in the body. To be *HIV-* is to have no HIV antibodies in the body, meaning that the virus is not present. It normally takes about three months after infection for antibodies to show up in blood tests. HIV is normally passed on via anal or vaginal sex without condoms (see **barebacking**), sharing needles or blood transfusions with infected blood. In rarer cases, HIV can be passed via oral sex, usually when the passive partner has bleeding gums, cuts or mouth ulcers.

homie-sexual noun: a gay rap/hip-hop fan who is also in the **closet**. US. Also *homo-thug*.

homocentric adjective: to be very concerned with homosexuality, perhaps to the point of erasure of heterosexuality.

homoerotic adjective: something which contains a subtext that could be interpreted as sexy by gay men. For example, the naked wrestling between Oliver Reed and Alan Bates in the film *Women in Love* (1969) could be read as homoerotic.

homogenic adjective: a term synonymous with *homosexual*, suggested by Edward Carpenter (1844–1929) in his 1895 book *Homogenic Love and its Place in a Free Society*. Carpenter defended love between men as innate and therefore natural.

homo in training noun: a young man or teenager who displays certain traits that suggest that he will eventually live a gay lifestyle. 'Little Calum knows all the dance moves to Madonna's Vogue. There goes another homo in training.' Also *to be one of tomorrow's men*.

homophile adjective: homosexual. Popular in the US in the 1950s although became unpopular with the onset of Gay Liberation in the 1970s. Derived from the Greek word *philos* meaning love.

homophobia noun: 1. an irrational fear of homosexuality. 2. an aversion or hatred of gay people, their lifestyle or culture, including behaviour based on this aversion. Coined by George Weinberg, the term first appeared in print in 1969. Weinberg discussed it at length in his book *Society and the Healthy Homosexual* (1972). Critics have observed that the term is problematic in that homophobia is not a phobia in the sense of claustrophobia or agoraphobia – so homophobics do not manifest physiological reactions to homosexuality. Also, the term implies that the problem exists at the individual, clinical level, rather than framing it as a social phenomenon which is based on intergroup relationships and cultural norms. See also **heterosexism**, **internalized homophobia**.

homophobic adjective: something which is prejudiced against gay men and lesbians.

homophobe noun: a person who possesses homophobic beliefs. Research comparing people who have favourable attitudes towards homosexuals with those who have negative attitudes has shown that homophobes tend to be male, older, less well-educated, living in areas where such negative attitudes represent the norm (e.g. rural areas or the Midwestern or Southern states in the US), more likely to attend religious services, endorse orthodox religious beliefs (such as the literal truth of the Bible), be politically conservative, psychologically authoritarian, supportive of traditional gender roles and less sexually permissive. See also **internalized homophobia**.

homosexual noun: a term coined by Karl Maria Kertbeny in the 1860s as a preference to the existing word that was used at the time to describe men who had sex with other men: *pederast*. Kertbeny claimed that many homosexuals were more masculine than other men, being superior to *heterosexuals*. He hoped that the word would help to eliminate the oppressive Paragraph 175 (see **hundred and seventy fiver**) in Germany. However, the word was instead adopted by doctors, including Richard von Krafft-Ebing who concluded that homosexuality was a form of inherited mental illness, resulting in effeminacy. This 'sickness' model dominated western opinions about men who had sex with other men for the first half of the twentieth century. By the early 1970s the word *homosexual,* with its medical connotations was superseded by the term *gay*.

homosexual panic noun: 1. a form of defence used in trials of men accused of harming or killing gay men. The belief being that the victim made a 'pass' at the attacker, who was so horrified that he went into 'homosexual panic' and violently lashed out. In the past this defence has been used to reduce the sentences of those who have committed homophobic hate-crimes. 2. the fear of being homosexual.

homovestite noun: someone who obsessively wears clothing of their own sex – the opposite of a **transvestite**.

hoop 1. noun: the anus, often derogatory e.g. 'Oh get away from me, you smelly hoop!' 2. verb: to fuck.

horizontal hood noun: a horizontal piercing of the clitoral hood.

horny adjective: 1. sexually aroused. 2. attractive.

horny porny noun: pornography.

horrorgy noun: an orgy that goes horribly wrong, e.g. ending in a jealous fight or being unexpectedly interrupted by an elderly family member.

hot monogamy noun: a late 1990s philosophy that sex in a gay long-term, monogamous relationship could be just as good or better than non-monogamous sex or cruising.

house noun: a close knit group of gay friends or **drag queens**. African-American slang. See **house mother**.

house mother noun: the authority figure who oversees a **family** of **drag queens** or gay men. African-American slang.

hum noun: humiliation during **BDSM** sex. Internet slang.

humpy adjective: very attractive and sexually desirable.

hundred and seventy fiver noun: a homosexual. From paragraph 175 of the German Penal Code of 1871 which outlawed homosexual practices. Originally *hundert-funf-und-siebziger*.

hundred dollar millionaire noun: someone who acts as if they're very wealthy when they aren't.

hung adjective: 1. having a large penis. See **well-hung**. 2. the size of the penis: 'he was hung like a field mouse'.

hunt dog noun: a boring lover.

husband noun: 1. a policeman. 2. any man who has the potential of being more than just a sexual dalliance.

hustler noun: a male prostitute. Also *call boy, dilly boy, escort, he-whore, kept boy, midnight cowboy, rent boy*.

HWP adjective: personal advertising acronym for *Height/ Weight Proportionate*.

I

ice-queen noun: a distant, rather cold gay man who acts in a superior manner.

important adjective: something which one *thinks* will help enhance one's social standing. 'I'm wearing my important clothes for this interview.'

I'm resting vocative: polite euphemism used in **bath-houses** to indicate that you aren't interested in having sex with someone.

in adjective: the preference of having a **trick** come to the house for sex.

ingulfing verb: inserting objects inside the anus.

intermediate sex noun: one of the earlier words to describe men who had sex with men. The term was popularlized by Edward Carpenter in the UK and the US and Magnus Hirschfeld in Germany. The belief being that homosexuals belonged to a third biological sex which stood mid-way between male and female. Also *third sex*.

internalized homophobia noun: 1. a closeted gay or bisexual person who hates or fears some or all aspects of homosexuality. Research published by Professor Henry Adams in the *Journal of Abnormal Psychology* in 1996 found that 80 per cent of 'exclusively heterosexual' homophobic men got erections when watching videos of gay men having sex, suggesting that their **homophobia** stems from a fear of exposure – such men are not as heterosexual as they would like others to believe. 2. other cases of internalized homophobia can occur when **out** gay men or lesbians complain about **sissies**, **drag queens**, **leathermen** etc., or hold prejudiced or discriminatory attitudes towards homosexuals, e.g. being against the idea that gay men can be parents, serve in the armed forces, or teach children.

intersexed adjective: a person born with male and female reproductive organs. Every year thousands of babies are born intersexual, and in the past some doctors have reshaped their genitals, without the consent or knowledge of the parents involved.

in the life adjective: euphemism for gay.

Iris adjective: irritated. From **Gayle**.

IRL adjectival phrase: internet acronym for *In Real Life*, as opposed to **cyber**.

Isabella noun: a deep piercing of the clitoral shaft.

ISO verb: personal advertising acronym for *In Search Of*.

issues noun: problems or concerns. 'I have dinner issues' means 'I'm about to eat'.

it's (always) all about ... adjectival phrase: 1. used to indicate that someone is selfish or self-absorbed: 'Why is it always all about you?' 2. completely obsessed: 'He's been all about Malcolm since last year.' Originally derived from the film *All About Eve* (1950).

it's (so) over vocative: it's no longer fashionable.

J

Jack and Jill party noun: a type of **circle jerk** party popular in the 1980s where both lesbians and gay men were invited.

jack-off, JO verb: to masturbate. Used at least as early as the 1950s. US. Also *Barclays* (UK), *beat-off, beat the meat, bring off, bust a nut, crank the shank, fist-glaze, five-fingered* *shuffle, flog the bishop, frig, hand gig, hand job, hand shandy, jerk off, make soup, Miss Fist, onanism, play solitaire, pound the pud, smack the pony, toss, toss off, unload, wank* (UK), *whack, whip the weasel, yank.*

jack-off club, jack-off party noun: a sex party, usually where video pornography is available and nudity is required. The main (or only) sexual act permitted is masturbation (or in some cases mutual masturbation).

jam noun: acronym for *Just A Man,* referring to a heterosexual man.

jean queen noun: a gay man who likes to wear denim jeans and prefers his partners to do the same. See **denim scene**.

jelly bean augery noun: a form of predicting who you will **trick** with, when cruising. US slang. A person buys a portion of jelly beans from a vending machine. The colours of the jelly beans represent the probability of ending up with a certain type of man, the more beans of a certain colour, the greater the chance. Black = a black man, white = a white man or **gym bunny**, yellow = an asian man, red = a Native American, green = a man with a beard, orange = a versatile, laid-back man, blue = a man with a swimmer's build, pink = a **twink**, violet = a camp man. The game can be modified, for example, by taking a handful of sweets from a packet of M+Ms or Smarties.

joanie, J adjective: glamorous. From the actress Joan Collins who epitomized 1980s decadent glamour in the US soap *Dynasty*.

john noun: the client of a prostitute.

jousting verb: a form of locker-room **homoerotic** play between two heterosexual men where erect penises are used as jousts and are aimed at each other's penis, pubic area and belly button.

Judge Judy noun: a nickname for a gay man who constantly judges other people's sexual behaviour. Derived from the US television programme of the same name.

just gay enough adjective: coined by *New York* magazine in 2000, to refer to a heterosexual man who is masculine, yet sensitive and interested in interior design.

K

K9 adjective: personal advertising acronym for *Canine* or someone who is interested in bestiality. The original K9 was a mechanical dog in the UK sci-fi series *Dr Who*.

k-hole noun: a disoriented or hallucinatory state or 'high' as the result of taking **Special K**.

key code noun: a way of signifying particular preferences by wearing keys on a key-ring attached to a belt-loop. In some contexts this will signify that the wearer is interested in **BDSM**. Keys worn on the left indicate a **top**, while they are worn on the right for a **bottom**. See also **hanky code**.

kicky adjective: a lot of fun.

king noun: the most dominant or outstanding lesbian in a particular area.

kink friendly adjective: someone who, while not interested in forms of sex such as **BDSM** or **D&S**, is still sympathetic and supportive of those who wish to do so. Also used to describe businesses which sell clothing to **leathermen**.

kinky adjective: an umbrella term applying to non-vanilla forms of sex such as **leather, BDSM, D&S, shrimping, watersports** etc.

Kinsey six adjective: totally gay. From the scale developed by Alfred Kinsey in *Sexual Behaviour in the Human Male* (1948). Can also be shortened to *six*. A *Kinsey zero* indicated someone who was totally heterosexual. Kinsey's scale popularized the notion that sexuality could be measured on a linear scale, with gradients of desire, rather than as a binary construct of homo- or hetero-. Kinsey put the number of men who are life-long homosexuals at 4 per cent, while the figure for those who were 'exclusively homosexual for at least three years between the ages of sixteen and fifty-five' was at 10 per cent.

kissing fish noun: lesbians, derogatory.

koala bear noun: a **bear** with light or blonde body hair.

koffiemoffie noun: a white air steward working for the South African airways during the apartheid period. From **Gayle**.

kool-aid lips noun: lipstick from the previous evening that won't come off. **Drag queen** slang, quoted in Darrin Hagen's *The Edmonton Queen* (1997). Left-on mascara is known as *racoon eyes*.

KY noun: a brand of water-based lubricant, often used to facilitate anal sex.

L

lace bear noun: a **bear** who calls his male friends 'girlfriend'.

laddie or lassie noun: children with gay parents. Originally this term had a negative connotation, assuming that the child would also 'turn out gay', but has more recently been reclaimed and can be used as a code allowing children to identify each other in public.

ladyboy noun: Usually a young East Asian male to female transsexual.

lamb noun: the (usually younger and inexperienced) partner of a **wolf**.

lambda noun: the eleventh letter of the Greek alphabet and the symbol of kinetic energy in physics. Used as a symbol by the **Mattachine Society** denoting homosexuality since the 1970s. It was employed as a symbol of justice and believed that one of the armies of the Greek city states used to paint the lambda on their shields – members of Greek armies are traditionally believed to have taken male lovers.

lamb to the slaughter noun: a nickname for someone new to the gay **scene** who becomes romantically involved with a predatory, experienced gay man, whose prime objectives are sexual conquest and validation. This generally ends in tears.

LDR noun: acronym for *Long Distance Relationship*.

LDU noun: acronym for *Leather/Denim/Uniform* as a fetish, popular with masculine, **straight-acting** gay men. Personal advertising slang.

lean cuisine queen noun: a gay man who diets.

leather noun: 1. leather clothing (see **leatherman**). 2. a synonym for **S&M**.

leather bear noun: a **bear** who is into **leather**.

leather family noun: a surrogate, adult-only 'family' comprised of people (largely gay and lesbian, but also increasingly open to bisexuals and heterosexuals) who embody the traditions and ethics of the leather scene.

leather purse noun: an aging (usually financially secure) gay man who's been on the receiving end of too many sun-bed treatments.

leatherman noun: a (usually gay) man whose appearance is based on wearing the following items of clothing: black leather jacket, trousers or chaps, boots, black leather cap. Also incorporates leather bondage gear such as wrist and arm bands and a torso harness.

leatherwoman noun: a female who is into the **leather** scene. Lesbian leatherwomen can also be referred to as *leatherdykes*.

lesbian noun: a gay woman. Derived from the name of the island of Lesbos, home of the Ancient Greek Sappho (born around 630 BC) whose poems celebrated love between women. Doctors helped to propel the term into popular usage in the late nineteenth century. Also *carpet muncher, dike, gaychick, leg-licker, lesbean, muff diver, slack, vagitarian, woman in comfortable shoes, woman-loving-woman.*

lesbian bed death noun: term used to describe the cessation of sexual activities between two women in a long-term relationship.

lesbian invisibility noun: the assumption that homosexuality only refers to gay men, resulting in the erasure of lesbians from representations of homosexuality. While it could be argued that lesbian invisibility has resulted in **homophobia** being directed more often at gay men, for example, it has never been illegal in the UK, it has also meant more recently that lesbians have been excluded or sidelined by the media, mainstream society and the gay scene.

lesbian stowaway noun: a **f-t-m transsexual** who tries to become a lesbian.

lesbyterian haircut noun: a short haircut stereotypically worn by some lesbians. See also **mud-flap hairdo**.

Lettie noun: a lesbian. From **Gayle**. See also the **Polari** entry for *lettie*.

let your hair down verb: to **come out**.

library noun: an adult bookstore.

lifestyle (the) noun: refers to *the leather lifestyle*, meaning the community of people who are part of the **leather family**. See **lifestyler**.

lifestyler noun: someone who has incorporated a **bottom** or **top** role into their everyday way of life. These relationships have gone beyond occasional roleplay. Many lifestylers are not in **the lifestyle** in that they are not participants in any organized or community **BDSM** or

D&S scene but conduct their relationships in privacy, at home.

lifestyle slave noun: a **slave** who has made a **24/7** commitment to a **master**, going beyond the realm of occasional sexual encounters and entering daily life.

lightbulb noun: a fat, bald **gym queen**.

lilies of the valley noun: haemorrhoids.

limits noun: a basic set of (usually physical) limits which are set by a **bottom** prior to **BDSM** role-play. For example, a 'pain limit' may rule out whipping, **blood-sports** etc. *Hard limits* are the maximum edge of a negotiated limit – for example, an allergy to rubber may make using clothing or toys made of rubber a hard limit. Limits may also be *pushed* or *stretched* over time. This commonly occurs when a bottom believes their limits stem from irrational fears and hopes they can be overcome with the help of the **top**.

limp wrist noun: one of the stereotypical characteristics of a gay man.

lineman noun: a **chub** who has more muscle than fat.

lip-lubed adjective: something which has been lubricated using saliva.

lipstick butch noun: a woman who wears stereotypically feminine clothing but behaves in a masculine way.

lipstick lesbian noun: 1. a feminine lesbian who may be in the **closet**. 2. a woman who wears her lesbian status like lipstick – it can be removed.

living doll noun: 1. a young, attractive gay man. 2. a type of **gimp**.

load noun: semen produced during a man's ejaculation.

locker room queen noun: a gay man who spends a long time getting changed and showering when visiting the gym, so he can cruise and stare at other guys.

LOL verb phrase: **cyber** acronym for *Laughing Out Loud.*

lollipop stop noun: a rest stop on a highway used for **cruising**.

long winded adjective: someone who takes a long time to ejaculate when being fellated.

love dart noun: 1. a large clitoris. 2. a small penis.

love Jones noun: an incredibly strong feeling of desire for someone.

lover noun: a long-term partner. Also *bf, boyf, boyfriend, fella, him indoors, husband, partner,* **significant other**.

low femme noun: a **femme** lesbian who may wear jeans and t-shirts rather than the skirts which are traditionally worn by **high femmes**. Also known as *blue jeans femme.*

LP noun: acronym for *Lesbian Potential,* used when attempting to discern whether or not someone is a lesbian.

LTR noun: acronym for *Long Term Relationship.*

lube noun: a shortened form of *lubrication,* used for ease during penetrative sex.

lucky Pierre noun: 1. a third person who makes up a **threesome** with two men in a relationship (therefore likely to receive the most attention). 2. a person in a threesome who gets fucked and fucks someone simultaneously.

lunch noun: 1. an attractive man. Also can be used as an adjective: *lunchy*. 2. a short version of **lunchbox**. 3. a 1970s UK gay magazine.

lunchbox noun: a man's crotch area. Also *packet*.

luppies noun: acronym for *Lesbian Urban Professionals*.

M

M2M noun: man to man.

m8 noun: internet slang for *mate*.

m80 noun: internet slang for *matey*.

M&M, MM noun: mutual masturbation. Also *play chopsticks*, derived from the crossing of hands when playing the tune *Chopsticks* on a piano.

macho adjective: masculine or tough.

macho slut noun: a woman or male **bottom** who is sexually aggressive.

make a milk run verb: to go to a public convenience for the purposes of sex.

male symbol noun: a circle with an arrow pointing upward towards the top right. Two symbols joined together indicate homosexuality. Two male symbols joined with two **female symbols** indicate the gay and lesbian community.

mama bear noun: a female security guard or policewoman.

Manto haircut noun: Manto's is a gay bar in Manchester, UK. A Manto haircut is worn by young, fashion-conscious gay men who use the bar.

map of Africa noun: a semen stain made on the bed-sheets after sex.

Mardi-Gras noun: a festival for gay men and lesbians with a carnival atmosphere. Mardi-Gras means *Fat Tuesday* and first came to New Orleans through its French heritage in 1699. See **pride**.

maricón noun: **faggot**, from Spanish.

mariposa noun: a male homosexual, from the Spanish for *butterfly*.

Martha adjective: 1. to be the passive partner during anal intercourse. 2. gay. See **Arthur or Martha**.

Mary-Sue noun: a generic narrator or non-famous person in **slash** fiction. For example, in a fictional story which describes how Brad Pitt rescued someone from a car accident, took them back to an isolated farm and had sex with them, the other person would be the Mary-Sue character, who the reader would be expected to identify with. Mary-Sue characters are usually flawless.

master noun: 1. a person who plays the dominant role in **BDSM** sexual roleplay. It is usual for masters and **mis-**

tresses to have **power-exchange** relationships with their partners, unlike **tops**. 2. a person in a long-term relationship with a submissive **slave**. Also *fuck master*.

Mattachine Society noun: Prior to what came to be known as Gay Liberation, the most well-documented vehicle for gay rights was the **homophile** movement, represented by organizations founded in the 1950s, the American Mattachine Society and the **Daughters of Bilitis**, which attempted to present homosexuality as a basic character trait, different from heterosexuality, yet admittedly one which was possessed by a minority. This difference was not celebrated, but instead, homophiles pleaded for tolerance, and acceptance/admittance of homosexuals on humanitarian grounds into mainstream society. One advert which describes the standpoint of the Mattachine Society reads 'Homosexuals are different ... but ... we believe that they have the right to be. We believe that the civil rights and human dignity are as precious as any other citizen ... we believe that the homosexual has the right to live, work and participate in a free society. Mattachine defends the rights of homosexuals and tries to create a climate of understanding and acceptance.' Members of the Mattachine Society were respectable and restrained, wearing suits and ties on marches, in contrast to the **GLF** activists and drag queens of the 1970s.

maul noun: an unsolicited or unwanted molestation by a **bear**. Bear slang.

mean queen noun: a gay man who likes to be a **top** in **BDSM** or **D&S** roleplay.

meanwhile vocative: a code meaning 'check out the attractive man over there'. US slang, as characterized in the film *The Broken Hearts Club* (2000).

meat noun: a penis (especially a large penis).

meat market noun: a place e.g. bar, gym or park where men cruise each other and/or have gay sex.

Mecca noun: a system of naming the cruising areas in a city or town. UK slang, derived from the Muslim place of worship. 'I was having no luck at Mecca 1 and then one of the regulars told me that he'd had some bona trade down at Mecca 2 so I thought I'd give it a try.'

member of the union noun: a lesbian.

Mexican nightmare noun: a kitsch or tacky decorating style involving mismatched colours. 'Have you seen Josh's new pad? It's a real Mexican nightmare!'

milk? vocative: used in response to someone who is being catty.

millionaire model genius noun: a gay man who has an exaggerated opinion of himself.

mind fuck noun: an extreme form of **head-play** where a **top** misleads a **bottom** into thinking that something terrible is about to happen to him or her.

Miss Congeniality noun: a sarcastic name for an unpleasant gay man.

Miss Julie noun: someone who, like Julie Newmar, has maintained their figure as they've aged.

Miss Thang pronoun: me. US **drag queen** slang. Sometimes used as a synonym for **Miss Thing**.

Miss Thing noun: 1. a form of address for a camp, outrageous or haughty gay man. 'Check out Miss Thing over there in the ostrich feather head-dress.' 2. the feminine side of all men. 3. a generic term of address used by a **drag queen** or gay man with lots of **attitude**.

mister sister noun: a fellow **drag queen**.

mistress noun: a female **master**.

mitten queen noun: a gay man who likes to masturbate other people.

MMMB noun: acronym for *Man-Man-Man Bop* – a gay **threesome**. Named after the song 'Mmmmbop' by the group Hanson.

MOMD noun: acronym for *Man Of My Dreams*.

Mona noun: money. From **Gayle**.

monarchy noun: any group of gay men.

Monet noun: someone who looks better from a distance.

money shot noun: the moment of male orgasm in a porn film. The money shot is seen as one of the most necessary elements of the movie and in some cases the actor will not be paid unless he is able to orgasm onscreen.

monosexism noun: the belief that it is better to stick to partners from one sex (whether you're heterosexual or homosexual). Monosexists may disapprove of bisexuals or dismiss them as 'confused'. See also **biphobia**.

monosexual noun: someone who is either exclusively homosexual or heterosexual.

MOR noun: acronym for *Mixed Orientation Relationship* referring to a relationship between two people of different sexualities – for example, a heterosexual woman and a gay man, or a lesbian and a bisexual man.

motel time noun: the last few minutes before a bar closes. 'Have you noticed how pretty everyone gets during motel time?'

mother gaga noun: an ageing, gossipy gay man.

motss noun: acronym for *members of the same sex*, derived from the name of a gay internet newsgroup.

Mr Man noun: an attractive, firm-bodied man. US **drag queen** slang.

MSM noun: *Men who have Sex with Men*. Derived via **HIV**-prevention groups in order to reach men who do not consider themselves to possess homosexual identities but engage in homosexual sex. This may cover closeted or married gay men, or men in countries such as Sri Lanka, India or Zimbabwe which have different definitions of sexual identity from those in westernized countries.

MSO noun: an acronym for *Male Sex Object*.

m-t-f, mtf, M2F adjective: an acronym for *male to female*, referring to a man who either wants to **cross-dress** as or become a woman. Also *queer queen, TGirl*.

mud-flap hairdo noun: a hairdo worn by some rural lesbians that is long and flat on the sides and short on top, so named after the hanging mud-flaps on diesel trucks.

muff noun: the female genitalia. Also *coochie, cooze, crack, cunt, fanny* (UK), *flap, flue, front bottom, gash, hole, minge, money-maker, other hole, pussy, quim, slash, slit, snatch, tail, twat, twot, vag.*

muff diving verb: performing cunnilingus. A *muff diver* or *muff diva* is slang for a lesbian.

muffin noun: an attractive gay man (usually young). Also *stud muffin.*

munch noun: 1. a group lunch in a public place where people who are interested in **BDSM** or **D&S** can meet for the first time or socialize with old friends in a safe, **vanilla** setting. From internet slang. 2. fellatio.

mundo adjective: large.

muscle bear noun: a **bear** who works out on a regular basis at the gym. Bear slang.

muscle muffin noun: an attractive gay man who is also muscular and short.

muscle queen noun: 1. a **gym queen**. 2. a gay man who prefers muscular men. Also *body queen.*

mwah vocative: exaggerated sound made when air-kissing someone.

N

nadbag noun: the scrotum. Also *nutsack, scrote.*

nasty adjective: used to describe extreme, intense or rough sex. The word has a positive evaluation. From gay porn slang: 'These hot guys get up to the nastiest action in our latest triple X video.'

nature/nurture noun: the question concerning whether homosexuals are born or made (although the debate stems from a wider one which attempts to find explanations for all forms of behaviour and personality – many researchers have concluded that both nature and nurture have a role to play). Eve Sedgewick in *Epistemology of the Closet* (1991: 40–4) points out that if either side 'wins' the argument, then it could have potential negative consequences for gay men and lesbians. For example – if it could be proven that there is such a thing as a gay gene (nature), then some groups may prompt research on attempts to change the gene, or homophobic parents may attempt to abort 'gay foetuses'. On the other hand, if homosexuality is found to be created by societal factors (nurture) then some societies may attempt to change in order to ensure that people did not become homosexual. Sedgewick notes 'We have all the more reason . . . to keep our understanding of gay origin . . . plural, multi-capillaried, argus-eyed, respectful and endlessly cherished.' See also **essentialism, gay brain, gay gene, social constructionism**.

navy cake noun: a gay sailor, especially one who is good-looking.

NAWW noun: acronym for *Not A Well Woman*.

NC noun: non-consensual sex. Internet slang.

neg adjective: **HIV** negative.

nellyectomy noun: an imaginary set of medical procedures carried out on a man in order to make him more camp or effeminate, for example: bones from the wrist are removed, making him limp-wristed. Used to describe how some gay men may be **straight-acting** in heterosexual company, but are happy to **camp it up** when they go into a gay bar.

neoconc noun: truncation of 'neo-conservative', a label formed by the group Sex Panic in order to denote a gay person who disapproves of gay promiscuity.

NEQ noun: a *Non-Equity Queen* – someone with an inflated opinion of himself. From *The Broken Hearts Club* (2000).

newbie noun: a gay man who has recently come out, usually one who is young and attractive. Newbies were originally people who were new to the internet in the 1990s, and therefore prone to making mistakes. Used to describe gay men in *The Broken Hearts Club* (2000). The more cynical term for a newbie is **lamb to the slaughter**.

new guard noun: a movement in the **leather** scene which updates **old guard** standards with more free-flowing and permissive attitudes towards lifestyle, for example embracing **pansexuality**. More typical of the attitudes of younger people on the scene. Also referred to as *next guard*.

new woman noun: a **m-t-f post-op transsexual**.

New Zealand sex noun: a form of **Australian sex** which does not include **rimming**.

night queen noun: a **drag queen** who only dresses in drag in the evenings to go out clubbing, or in private at home.

nipple tug-of-war noun: a **BDSM** game where two people put on **tit clamps** with chains running from one person to the other and lean backwards.

no! vocative: a reply upon hearing a piece of gossip, roughly translating as 'That's the most scandalous piece of information I've heard in ages, please tell me everything you know about this and then we can discuss it at length'. Also *shut up!*

no fats, femmes or flamers phrase: exclusionary, used in gay personal adverts. See also **straight-acting**.

non-biological noun: the gay or lesbian non-birth parent of a child, where the other partner is the biological parent of the child via a previous heterosexual relationship or by other means.

non-camp adjective: masculine. From gay personal advert slang. See **straight-acting**.

non-op noun: a **transsexual** who has decided not to have **gender reassignment surgery**, yet permanently dresses and acts in their desired gender role.

non-scene adjective: not using the commercial gay scene of pubs, bars, baths/saunas etc. Also *NSc*.

Nora adjective: stupid. From **Gayle**.

nullification noun: an extreme form of **body modification** involving voluntary amputation of body parts.

number noun: 1. an attractive person. 'Check out that number at the bar!' 2. a casual sex partner.

numbers game noun: a combination of oral and anal sex, represented by the numbers 66 and 69.

O

OGT noun: acronym for *Obviously Gay Trait*. For example, having a collection of Judy Garland albums, **clutching your pearls**, being picked last for team sports. Used in *The Broken Hearts Club* (2000).

OHAC noun: acronym for *Own Home Own Car*. Used in personal adverts.

OIF noun: acronym for *Occasional Intimate Friend*. An OIF is a non-romantic friend who also happens to be a sexual partner. However, unlike **fuck buddies**, there is a degree of caring and companionship involved in the relationship.

old girl noun: an elderly male homosexual.

old guard noun: the exclusively gay male organized network of **leather** clubs, existing in the 1940s and 1950s which established the traditions of the culture. The old guard had a regimented, almost militaristic approach to leathersex and created a close-knit community based on solidarity rather than diversity. Some old guard attitudes are seen as belonging to an older generation and thus outdated. However, the old guard is still held in reverence as a revolutionary movement. Many of its traditions still contain today, such as standards for dress or what constitutes an **S&M** relationship, and some people view these standards as the only pure model for the leather culture.

omnisexual adjective: someone who isn't limited about who or what they would have sex with.

oncer noun: a gay man who will only have sex once with someone.

one-eyed Cyclops noun: the head of the penis.

on fire adjective: to be *flaming*. See **flamer**.

on the down low adjective: appearing to be heterosexual in public, but having gay sex in private. US African-American slang.

on the rag adjective: to be in a bad mood. Originally slang referring to menstruation.

on the turn adjective: to change one's sexuality either from gay to straight or vice versa. UK.

open relationship noun: a long-term relationship where one or both partners are free to have sex with other people. Usually boundaries are stipulated such as: no emotional or romantic involvement with other parties and **safe sex** must be practiced. 'We have an open relationship, I tell Harry every time I'm unfaithful, but I don't brag about what a huge cock my trick had.'

open your purse verb: to break wind.

opera queen noun: a gay man who loves the opera or divas. A *theatre* queen is a gay man who loves musicals.

oreo noun: a black man who holds 'white' values. US. From the name of the biscuit – see also **oreo sex**. Derogatory. Also *fade*.

oreo sex noun: a **threesome** involving two black men and a white man. US. Derived from the Oreo snack: a creamy-coloured filling sandwiched between two dark pieces of biscuit.

orphan noun: a gay man who has just been dumped by his lover.

otter noun: a **bear** who possesses features such as hairiness or beard, but who has a slender build. Bear slang.

out 1. verb: to out someone is to reveal their sexuality to others without their consent. The UK gay rights pressure group *Outrage* were criticized for 'outing' eight gay bishops in 1994, although their leader, Peter Tatchell claims that they have never outed anyone, but rather asked them to 'tell the truth' about their sexuality. 2. adjective: to be open about your sexuality. See also **closet, come out**.

over-share verb: to reveal too much information about yourself, especially when it makes others feel uncomfortable.

Oz noun: 1. San Francisco. A reference to the film *The Wizard of Oz* (1939) which starred Judy Garland and is a favourite among many gay men. See also **friend of Dorothy**. 2. Any prison (from the US television series of the same name).

P

PA noun: 1. acronym for *Photo Appreciated*. From personal advertising slang. 2. a **Prince Albert**.

packing verb: 1. wearing a strap-on dildo or something resembling a penis-like bulge in the underwear (females). See **gender fuck**. 2. wearing any sort of padding e.g. a rolled-up sock to make the penis appear bigger (males).

padding noun: undergarments which contain foam, used by **transgendered** people, allowing the body to appear more masculine or feminine. See **gender fuck**.

pain slut noun: an extreme masochist (not someone who is necessarily sexually promiscuous). Also *pain pig*.

paint verb: to apply make-up. **Drag queen** slang.

pain threshold noun: a limit where pain ceases to be pleasurable for a **bottom**.

Pandora noun: an inquisitive gay man. From **Gayle**.

Pandora's box noun: a very promiscuous gay man who is well known for possessing (and passing on) sexually transmitted diseases: 'Oh don't go with Simon, he's a regular Pandora's box!' UK slang. From the Greek legend – Pandora, a mortal woman was given a mysterious box to look after by the god Mercury. Despite being told not to, she opened the box and unleashed all the diseases, sorrows, vices and crimes that afflict humanity.

pansexuality noun: all types of sexuality. For example, this word could be used to refer to the expansion of **BDSM**, **D&S** and **leather** communities to include not only gay men, but also lesbians, bisexuals and heterosexuals. A pansexual event would welcome people of all sexual orientations. The word also refers to celebrating links between different types of sexual fetishes, uniting them in order to enable civil rights campaigns, or to educate the '**vanilla**' public about the diversity and consensuality of other forms of sex.

pansexual play noun: when people of different sexualities engage in non-sexual **BDSM** roleplay together. For example a heterosexual man may spank a gay man, although he would not consider having a sexual or romantic relationship with him.

pansy without a stem noun: a lesbian.

panty doll noun: a **transvestite** who finds wearing female underwear to be especially cathartic.

panty training noun: a form of **forced feminization** when a **top** 'forces' a **bottom** to wear female underwear and lingerie in order to cross-dress and humiliate him. *Petticoat training* or *petticoating* is a form of panty-training using ruffled slips.

party favours noun: drugs.

passing verb: 1. being perceived by others as a member of the opposite sex when **cross-dressing**. The adjectival form is *passable*. 2. being perceived as heterosexual, when actually gay.

passive adjective: receptive anally. Also *bitch, bottom, buey, catcher, get one's tail done, main queen, Martha, pillow biter, taker*.

PC dyke noun: acronym for *Politically Correct Dyke* – a lesbian who uses language carefully so as not to offend minority groups.

pearl necklace noun: semen which has been ejaculated onto the neck and/or chest of a partner. Also *jelly jewellery*.

percussion play noun: all types of striking such as caning, flogging, paddling, slapping, and whipping.

Peter Pan noun: a gay man in his 50s or older who still acts like a teenager.

phone sex noun: the act of talking about sex or describing fantasies over the telephone, often accompanied by masturbation.

PIB noun: acronym for *Person In Black*.

piece noun: an attractive man.

pince adjective: pointy or sharp. UK rare.

Pines (the) noun: slang for Fire Island Pines, a gay male summer beach colony founded in the 1950s a mile up the beach from **Cherry Grove** on **Fire Island**.

ping verb: a variant of **gaydar** where one **transgendered** or **cross-dressing** person detects another in public.

pink part (the) vocative: kiss my ass.

pink pound, pink dollar noun: gay men and lesbians are considered to be an attractive form of *niche marketing* as they are thought to be wealthy, fashionable and brand loyal. Gay men in particular are believed to have relatively large disposable incomes. However, studies which have supported these views have tended to focus on openly gay consumers who hold credit cards and donate to political causes. Other studies have found that gay men tend to earn smaller than average incomes. For example, a US study published by Lee Badgett in 2001 found that the average gay male earned about 17 per cent less per year than the average heterosexual male. This finding was reiterated in the UK in a *Gay Times* survey of readers in 1998 which put the average reader yearly income at £14,969, compared to the national average of £16,000. Despite such findings, it may be true that some gay men and lesbians have higher disposable incomes than their heterosexual counterparts because of fewer family commitments.

pink triangle noun: an inverted triangle that gay men were forced to wear in Nazi concentration camps in World War II. Later it was adopted by the gay community as a symbol of pride. See **black triangle**.

pinky ring noun: a ring that is worn on the little finger of the left hand as a signifier of homosexuality. See **wedding ring**.

pipe man noun: a **butch** man who incorporates pipe smoking into his sexual play. See **cigar daddy**.

piss-elegant adjective: the belief that someone is socially superior to others, especially when they aren't. 'She was such a piss-elegant queen with her opera and her wine tasting, but it turned out that she sold broken biscuits down the market.'

pit job noun: any sexual act where someone's armpit is the focus of attention.

play noun: **BDSM** slang to describe a kinky encounter. From *roleplay*. A *player* is someone who has experience of the **leather** or **BDSM** lifestyle, while *heavy* or *hardcore players* prefer intense **S&M**.

playa noun: someone with a large ego who has numerous sexual relationships. US.

play checkers verb: to move from one seat to another in an adult movie theatre, in the hope that someone will be found to have sex with.

play partner noun: 1. any partner during a **BDSM** encounter. 2. someone who is only seen for casual or kinky sex, rather than a romantic involvement. See **fuck buddy**.

play piercing noun: a form of radical (often ritual) **S&M** play where pins, needles or other piercing implements are inserted into the flesh.

play space noun: any space used in **BDSM** roleplay. Also *playroom*, **dungeon**.

plucky 1. noun: a gay man who plucks his eyebrows. 2. adjective: the behaviour of a **drama queen** who likes to milk pity out of his friends by relating stories of how, despite being an attentive lover, he's been betrayed by scores of partners, but has somehow attempted to 'keep smiling through the tears'.

plucky anthem: any song which embodies aspects of a **plucky** 'I've been hurt but life must go on' mindset. For example: 'I Will Survive', 'Alone Again, Naturally', 'All By Myself', 'You Don't Send Me Flowers Anymore' and 'What Kind of Fool Am I?'.

PLWA noun: acronym for *Person Living With AIDS*. Also **PWA**.

PNP, P/P verb: acronym for *party and play*, itself a euphemism to describe drugs and sex.

pocket pool noun: obvious masturbation while wearing pants or trousers. 'This awful guy came up to me and started playing pocket pool so I said, "Do you have a problem with your trousers?"'

polar bear noun: a mature **bear** with greying or white hair. **Bear** slang.

poly adjective: polygamous, having more than one partner.

ponyboy, ponygirl noun: a **bottom** during **animal training** roleplay. Also *puppy*.

poof, poofter, puff noun: a gay (usually effeminate) man. UK. Derogatory.

poppers noun: the chemical substance amyl nitrate (and also its close relatives butyl nitrate and isobutyl nitrate). Amyl is a vasodilator – it causes blood vessels to open wider allowing blood to flow more freely and temporarily increases the pulse rate. Originally amyl nitrate was inhaled from glass capsules that broke open with a 'pop' – hence the name. Poppers became popular on the gay scene from the 1970s onwards, inhaling them during sex produced a somewhat disorienting yet pleasant rush. Poppers also help to relax the sphincter muscles during anal sex. In the early days of **AIDS**, some people suspected that poppers may have been the cause of Karposi's sarcoma, or even AIDS, as a proportion of the people who were first diagnosed had also used poppers. However, this link was disproven. While there is evidence that poppers do lower immune functions, the body is believed to be able to recover after a few days. With that said, sniffing poppers can also cause the blood vessels in the anal lining to become enlarged, which may facilitate **HIV** infection if condoms are not used. The rush provided by poppers may also release inhibitions for some users, making them not as careful about safe sex as they otherwise would be.

porn star name noun: a person's porn star name is derived from the name of their first pet (or favourite animal as a child), coupled with their mother's maiden name. See **camp name, drag queen name**.

post-op transsexual noun: a **transsexual** who has undergone surgery to change his or her sex and lives as a member of the opposite sex. See **pre-op transsexual**.

potato queen noun: a gay man who has a fetish for Irish men. UK. Derogatory.

poundcake queen noun: a gay man who likes to be defecated on. See also **brown shower**.

power exchange noun: a situation where power is consensually transferred from a **top** to a **bottom** during **BDSM** or **D&S** roleplay.

power lesbian noun: a sophisticated, wealthy, professional lesbian. The female equivalent of an **A-Gay**.

poz adjective: to have tested **HIV**-positive.

pre-cum noun: fluid which oozes from the penis, prior to orgasm.

pre-op transsexual noun: a **transsexual** who is yet to have sexual reassignment surgery but may have taken some steps towards changing his or her sex, for example: hormone therapy, breast implants or removal, plastic surgery or electrolysis. See **post-op transsexual**.

pretty boy noun: an attractive young male.

pretty police noun: young, attractive policemen who play the part of gay bait in an ambush of cruising areas. Also **agent provacateur**, *decoy*, *fairy hawk*, *peep-hole shakers*, *urinal sniffers*.

prick tease, PT noun: someone who derives a thrill from cruising others, but has no intention of having sex.

pride noun: 1. a sense of empowerment about being gay. 2. a march or parade which is a celebration of homosexuality. In the UK at least, Gay Pride marches are beginning to be replaced by the more festival-oriented **Mardi-Gras**.

Prince Albert, PA noun: a genital piercing, entering the opening of the urethra, emerging from the underside of the glans and closed by a steel ball. Named after its most famous wearer, the husband of Queen Victoria. Also *PA*. The female equivalent is known as a *Princess Albertina*. See also **Queen Victoria**.

princess noun: a young man or teenager who has either just **come out** or is likely to grow up to be gay. Literally a 'future queen'. See also **homo in training**.

Princeton rub noun: sex between two men where one's penis rubs against the other's thighs. Named after the American University where this activity is said to have been popular. Also *college fuck, dry fuck, English method, Harvard Style, hump, irrumatio, leg fuck*.

process verb: to endlessly analyse and talk over a situation. Believed to be common among some lesbians involved in political-coalition work. Popular processing phrases are 'I hear you' and 'I respect that'.

prole troll noun: an unattractive working-class person.

pronoun game noun: the act of referring to people via opposite-sex pronouns or nouns, so 'she' becomes 'he' and vice versa. This can be done to indicate that someone is either gay, closeted or very camp. But it can also be used on heterosexual people – 'You'll have to act butch for the next few days, my father's coming to visit and you know what *she* thinks of my interesting lifestyle!' Additionally the pronoun game can be used when someone tries to hide their sexuality from heterosexual people who they don't want to **come out** to. See also **hell-sparking the pronoun**.

PT noun: acronym for *Profile Trap* – someone who is attractive from one angle only.

public sex noun: sex which occurs in a public or semi-private setting such as a **cottage**, **back room**, **bath-house** or **cruising area**. The lack of privacy may mean that others can observe or join in.

punishment noun: the act of been penetrated either orally or anally by a very large penis.

purple star noun: an enamel symbol worn by some lesbians in the 1970s.

push button noun: a contact which is used by gay men in a new town in order to find others.

pushy sub noun: 1. a joking term for a **bottom** or submissive who likes to act naughty in order to be 'punished' from a **top**. 2. a bottom who is so unruly that he/she turns the top off. Also *greedy sub*.

pussy noun: 1. a man's anus. 2. a man's penis. Originally sexual slang meaning *vagina*, the word crossed over into gay slang and is generally used to refer to a passive gay man, sometimes during **BDSM** sex.

pussy quivers noun: a pleasurable, expectant feeling in the anus, just before being fucked.

put one's foot in the pot verb: to cook a tasty meal. 'You really put your foot in the pot with that vegetable lasagne.'

pvt noun: a truncation of *private,* used in internet chatrooms to refer to a one-to-one private chat.

PWA noun: acronym for *Person With AIDS*. See **PLWA**.

Q

Q cards noun: gay 'calling cards', usually containing symbols or phrases below the name. The internet-based **bear code** and its variants are a modern form of Q card.

quaggot noun: a truncation of *queer faggot.*

queen noun: any gay man. See also the **Polari** entry.

queen bee noun: 1. this term is often used derisively to describe a socially dominant or assertive gay man. A queen bee often has money, an entourage and many sexual partners. Note the 1955 film of the same name, starring **gay icon** Joan Crawford. Also *mother*. 2. a **fag hag**.

queen bitch noun: 1. a purely evil, selfish, flamboyant gay man or drag queen. Typical queen bitch behaviour includes: stealing someone's boyfriend, putting drugs in someone's drink 'for a laugh', or leaving their friends alone and without a ride home in a club if they manage to trick someone into taking them home for the night. 2. a gay man or drag queen who likes to pretend to be a bitch, but only for comic effect.

queen for a day noun: a married (or otherwise 'heterosexual') man who will occasionally have gay sex.

queen of clubs noun: a gay man who loves clubbing. Also *club queen, disco dolly*.

queen of denial noun: a gay man who is unable to admit something to himself and/or others. 'Well of course I'm happy for Bob now he's hooked up with James. Oh who am I kidding? I'm such a queen of denial!'

queen of scotch noun: an alcoholic gay man.

queen of spades noun: an African-American gay man.

queen out verb: to act outrageously gay or camp, particularly in unusual circumstances. 'Frank really queened out at the wedding reception with his Cher impersonation.'

Queen Victoria noun: a urethral piercing which exits the top of the glans. Also known as a *reverse PA*. See **Prince Albert**.

queen without a country noun: a gay man who thinks he's popular, fashionable or witty but isn't.

queeny, queenly adjective: 1. flamboyantly gay. 2. haughty.

queer adjective: the word *queer* was used from about 1700 to refer to something which was bad or worthless. It had become a popular derogatory term for a homosexual by the early-mid twentieth century: 'he's queer as a three-penny bit', 'queer as a coot'. However, in the early 1990s *queer* was reclaimed by members of the gay community and given a more overtly political and academic slant. Growing out of earlier movements on identity politics *queer* came to stand for the concept of identities as being fluid, multiple, overlapping and interactive. *Queer* could mean gay, lesbian, bisexual, transgendered, black, Latino, working-class or a combination of any or all of the above at different times, as well as numerous other terms which were related to dispossessed or stigmatized minority groups. *Queer* was merely anything that was against the 'normal' or the 'dominant'. See Judith Butler's *Gender Trouble: Feminism and the Subversion of Identity* (1990) for more information.

queer bashing, queer baiting verb: engaging in a violent homophobic attack. See **basher**.

queer Bunter noun: an overweight, young, bespectacled gay man. UK slang. From the *Billy Bunter* series of books written by Frank Richards in the 1940s and 1950s.

Queer Nation noun: a US activist group. 'We're Here. We're Queer. Get used to it!'

queer straight noun: a heterosexual person who carries out activism on the behalf of the LGBT community, or one who does not conform to type.

quilt (the) noun: a commemorative quilt, comprising of many hundreds of six by three foot panels, each of which is a memorial to at least one person who has died of an AIDS-related illness.

R

rag trade, raggy noun: any gay man who works in a clothing shop or in the fashion industry. Derived from the UK 1960s/70s television sitcom *The Rag Trade*.

rainbow flag noun: a flag designed by Gilbert Baker in 1978, consisting of six horizontal bars of colour: red, orange, yellow, green, blue and violet, which has come to represent gay diversity and **pride** and is often hung outside gay homes or gay-friendly businesses. Originally the flag had eight stripes – but hot pink and indigo were dropped. Also *freedom flag*.

rainbow kiss noun: 1. vomit. 2. a kiss which is given to someone after you've just performed oral sex on them, retaining their semen in your mouth.

rake noun: a man of 'doubtful morality' in seventeenth century England. Rakes had sex with men and women but also had a reputation for being masculine and virile. Around 1700, the image of the rake was replaced with that of the more effeminate *molly*.

ranch adjective: crazy. US. Derived from Anita Bryant ranch-style 'homosexual healing centres'. 'Rhonda's said she'll go to the ranch if she can't get that frock in her size.'

reacharound noun: the act of masturbating your partner while you are fucking them. Considered to be 'good manners'. From gay porn slang.

reach under noun: to masturbate someone in an adjacent cubicle of a public toilet by putting your hand under the partition.

read verb: to (often publicly) unleash a string of unpleasant 'home truths' and insults upon someone. In noun form this is a *reading*. Also *pop your beads, read your beads, say a mouthful, string your beads*.

real time noun: actual sexual contact as opposed to **cyber**. Also *RT, R/T*.

reciprocate verb: to give a **blow job** to someone who has just fellated you.

reclaim verb: to use a pejorative word within a marginalized community in order to take away its power and give it a positive meaning. Examples of reclaimed words include *bitch, cunt, dyke,* and *queer.*

red ribbon noun: a small loop of ribbon attached to a lapel or shirt with a safety pin, signifying **AIDS** awareness and solidarity for people living with AIDS. Typically the price of the ribbon will go to an AIDS charity.

rent boy, rent noun: a male prostitute. More information in the **Polari** section.

re-op noun: a **post-op transsexual** who undergoes surgery to restore the features of his/her birth sex.

ret 2 go adjective: ready to go.

RFD queen noun: acronym for *Rural Free Delivery* – a gay man who lives in a small town or is from the countryside.

rice and potatoes noun: gay Asians (rice) and gay Caucasians (potatoes).

rice queen: noun 1. a gay Asian man. 2. a gay man who likes Asians. Derogatory. See **sticky rice queen**.

rim verb: to lick, tongue, kiss and penetrate the anus with the tongue. Also *analingus, ass kiss, ass lick, blow some ass, brown nose, eat jam, eat out, tongue.*

Rita noun: a **rent boy**. From **Gayle**.

road game noun: someone who goes hitching-hiking, or picks up hitch-hikers in the hope of it leading to gay sex.

rodeo verb: to have **kinky** sex.

role noun: an identity carried out during a sexual **scene**, often during **BDSM** or **D&S** sex. For example, **top** or **bottom, dom** or **sub**.

rough trade noun: a form of **trade** who becomes violent or demands money after sex.

rubber up verb: to wear a **condom**.

rubies noun: lips.

runway (the) noun: an area of Manhattan on 8th Avenue between 14th and 23rd streets.

runway dancing verb: dancing flamboyantly, while emulating the poise and attitude of a catwalk model.

Russian roulette party noun: a sex party without condoms where **HIV** positive and HIV negative men are present. Negative men take their chances that they will or won't be infected by having sex. The participants may or may not know the HIV status of any of the other participants in advance. From **barebacking** slang.

S

S&M, SM, sadomasochism, sadie-masie noun: the act of deriving pleasure from giving or receiving pain. Also *algolagnia.* Sadism (pleasure while inflicting pain) is derived from the name of the Marquis de Sade, while masochism (pleasure while experiencing pain) is named after the writer Leopold von Sacher-Masoch. See also **BDSM, leather, master, slave**.

S&M bar noun 1. a bar used by people who enjoy sadomasochism. 2. a 'stand and model' bar, populated by attractive young men who pose and act aloof.

safe, sane and consensual noun: ethical standards formulated by David Stein for **kinky** or **BDSM** sex. All activity should not cause harm, should respect the body and mind, and should be between adults who are able to give informed consent.

safe sex noun: any form of sexual activity which minimizes the possibility of exchange of body fluids, especially blood and/or semen, particularly in order to lessen the chance of **HIV** infection (although this is also applicable to other sexually transmitted diseases). For example: mutual masturbation, kissing, frottage or penetrative sex using a condom. It has been argued that the safest sex is no sex at all, so the concept should really be considered in terms of *safer sex*.

safe sex contract noun: 1. a written agreement, usually between two partners in a long-term **open relationship** where both parties promise to only engage in **safe sex** outside the relationship; the definition of what exactly constitutes safe sex being negotiated in advance. 2. a contract used by some gay **bath-houses** which requires patrons to promise to only engage in safe sex. Also *safe sex agreement*.

safe word noun: a code word or expression used in **BDSM** roleplay which gives a **bottom** the right to terminate the activity. Also called *safety code, stop code, stop word*. A *safe gesture* will be used if the bottom is incapable of speech e.g. because they are gagged.

salad queen noun: a gay man who likes to **rim**.

salt in your diet verb: to have sex with sailors.

SAM noun: acronym for *Smart Ass Masochist* – a **bottom** who will act feisty and verbally tease a **top** in order to get extra discipline.

sapphistry noun: lesbian love. Derived from the lesbian poet of ancient Greece, Sappho.

Sappho Daddy-O noun: a heterosexual man who enjoys the company of lesbians.

SASA adjective: acronym for *straight-acting, straight-appearing*. See **GAGA**.

sashay verb: to exaggerate stereotypically 'gay' mannerisms.

sash queen noun: someone who participates in **leather** contests and wins awards. This phrase is used by the **BDSM** community to jokingly refer to someone who is vain.

scat noun: 1. faeces. 2. the act of using faeces for sexual gratification e.g. enemas, **brown showers**, watching or being watched while defecating, being ordered to soil one's underwear or eating shit. Human faeces, unlike urine, contains bacteria which breaks down the food and turns it into waste. This bacteria remains alive after it is eliminated from the body, and can be extremely dangerous if consumed. Also *hot lunch*.

scene noun: 1. the commercial, physical aspect of the gay community, characterized by gay bars, nightclubs, saunas, restaurants, taxi firms etc. Derived from 1950s US beatnik and jazz slang referring to a place where people of common interests meet or where a particular activity is carried out. 2. a more specialized sexual or roleplay subculture: e.g. the leather scene. 3. a single encounter. 'We had a watersports scene and then I went home.' verb: 4. to carry out S&M. 'I'll be sceneing with him next week.'

scene queen noun: a gay man who lives for and on the gay **scene**.

scenery noun: an attractive, yet unavailable person (usually because their sexuality is incompatible). 'As we walked past the army training camp we enjoyed the scenery.'

scene space noun: the boundaries, both physical and emotional where **BDSM** roleplay takes place.

schwa noun: a cute guy.

scrap the clause, kill the clause verb phrase: a campaign referring to the repeal of **Clause 28** in the UK.

scrotum parachute noun: a pouch-like device, usually made of studded leather, which can have metal weights attached to it via a chain, or series of chains. The pouch is worn around the scrotum, causing the weights to pull down on it.

sea hag noun: someone who was once sun-tanned and beautiful, but has aged badly.

second-parent adoption noun: when a child is legally adopted by the same-sex partner of one of its biological parents. See also **laddie or lassie**.

secret sister noun: a **drag queen** or **transvestite** who keeps her cross-dressing as private as she can.

see Tarzan – hear Jane noun: the feeling of disappointment (or sometimes spiteful glee) upon encountering a man who has a fantastic body but then opens his mouth to reveal a camp or high-pitched voice.

serial monogamy noun: a pattern of how some lesbians conduct relationships – having a series of short yet intense and exclusive partnerships. This is often a stereotype, rather than a reality.

service-connected disability noun: a heterosexual man who finds out that he enjoys having gay sex while in the armed forces.

service-oriented top noun: a **top** who is very aware of a **bottom's** desires.

session noun: a sexual encounter (especially **BDSM**).

sex noun 1. erotic activity. 2. the categorization of a person as male or female according to their genitals. See also **gender**.

sex pig noun: usually a male **submissive bottom** in rough **BDSM** sex.

sex-positive dyke noun: a lesbian who is feminist, but doesn't think that enjoying penetration equals being a male-identified dupe.

shade noun: **attitude**. To have lots of attitude is to be *shady*. US.

shag bag noun: the bag a gay man takes out with him on an evening where he's hoping to **trick**. The bag contains toothbrush, clean underwear, clothes etc.

shag tag noun: a format used by gay nightclubs in the 1990s. Upon entering, patrons are given a sticker or badge to wear, which contains a unique number. When seeing someone attractive who you'd like to know better, rather than going up to chat with them, or spending the evening trying to make eye contact, you can simply clock their number and leave a private message for them on a board or with the DJ. Messages may be anonymous. 'Terry's pissed cos I got shag-tagged five times tonight, and nobody replied to *any* of the messages he left.'

sharps noun: anything used to cut or pierce the flesh in extreme **S&M** sex. For example, knives or razors.

shaver noun: a **m-t-f transgendered** person who shaves off her body and leg hair.

s/he, sie pronoun: used sometimes to refer to transgendered people. Also *hem, hes, hir, ir, per.*

shiny face noun: a gay man who wears too much moisturizer. UK.

shop door noun: the fly in a pair of trousers.

shore dinner noun: a gay man who likes to give oral sex to sailors.

short-arm inspection noun: a medical inspection (usually in the army or navy) of male genitals, in order to check for signs of sexually-transmitted diseases. Also *prick parade.*

shrimping verb: toe-sucking. A *shrimp queen* or *shrimper* is someone who gets off on sucking toes.

shut butt noun: an anus that is difficult to penetrate.

significant other, SO, sother. noun: a long-term same-sex partner. US.

sissie noun: 1. an effeminate gay man. 2. used by closeted US gay hiphop/rap fans known as **homie-sexuals** as a derogatory term directed at openly gay men. 'I'll let a sissie suck my dick, but I don't want to talk to him or hang out with him.' 3. a submissive male cross-dresser or one who is being **panty trained**. Also *sissie-slut*.

sissy-maid noun: a male, cross-dressed in a maid's uniform who serves a **top**. See also **French maid**.

six pack noun: 1. tight, defined abdominal muscles. 2. six cans of beer and therefore the anwer to the joke: 'What's the difference between a straight man and a gay man?'

sixty nine, 69 noun: mutual oral sex, occurring simultaneously. 'Sixty nine, sixty nine, I'll suck yours if you suck mine!'

sixty six, 66 noun: anal sex.

size queen noun: a gay man who prefers partners who are **well-hung**. 'Betty's such a size queen, she gets all misty-eyed when she sees a draught excluder.'

skag drag noun: a rough-and-ready attempt to put on **drag**, the result being that masculine characteristics are not well hidden. Also *dress-up, hag-drag, mop*.

skin, skinhead noun: the original skinheads were mostly heterosexual, working-class youths in the UK who wore Doc Marten boots, drainpipe denim jeans and check or polo shirts as well as shaving their heads. Since then, gay men who were into an ultra **straight-acting** look, or interested in **BDSM** have adopted this style.

slapper noun: northern UK gay slang for a promiscuous person.

slash noun: a form of erotic fiction, usually involving chronicling the sexual adventures of characters from existing films or television programmes. Slash is popular on the internet, and has earned its name from the way that relationships are noted via slashes e.g. m/m (gay male) or f/f (lesbian). One of the earliest forms of slash fiction involved an imagined ongoing sexual relationship between Kirk and Spock in *Star Trek*, and was serialized by women. See also **Mary-Sue**.

slave noun: a person who is sexually submissive. See also **BDSM, gimp, master**.

slave contract noun: a document created by a **top** and **bottom** in which the terms of their relationship are set out. Contracts are usually limited to a pre-agreed period of time, although some may vow a permanent commitment to each other. See **lifestyle slave**.

sleaze noun: usually a more extreme and dirty form of **kinky** sex.

sleeve noun: a device resembling a sheath, which can be used to cover a **vibrator**.

sling noun: a hammock-like contraption sometimes used in sex, particularly group sex. One person lies suspended in the sling, allowing him or her to be penetrated by others.

sloppy seconds noun: the experience of having sex with a man who has just been fucked by someone else. Also *pull a train, stirring the porridge.*

slow down Mary vocative: a warning given to someone who is misbehaving or going too far.

slush queen noun: a gay man of any ethnicity who is attracted to either black or white men. See also **dinge queen**, **snow queen**.

slut noun: 1. very promiscuous gay man or woman. Also *baggage, bike, bint, bitch in heat, brazen woman, doxy, fallen woman, floozy, harlot, hussy, jade, jezebel, loose woman, old bag, slag, slapper, slutbag, slutbitch, slutbitchwhore, tart, tramp, trash, trollop, vixen, wanton, whore, whorella, woman of the night*. 2. a ritual insult for a **bottom** during **BDSM** sex.

small fancier noun: someone who likes their partner to have a small penis. See **winkle**.

smooth adjective: having no body hair.

smurf noun: 1. a short gay man. 2. a young, blonde gay man with **attitude**. US.

snack noun: an attractive person. US.

snap noun: the snapping of fingers used to punctuate and accentuate speech, used by African-Americans. A *snap queen* is a gay man who is very good at snap.

snowball queen noun: someone who likes to exchange semen orally with a partner, after **sixty nining** him. See also **rainbow kiss**.

snow queen noun: 1. a non-white man who is attracted to white men. Also *snow-shoveller*. 2. a gay man who uses cocaine.

soaking verb: to admire the (male) scenery. UK. See **grazing**.

social constructionism noun: the theory that homosexuality is not innate, but a function of social conditioning – for example, via formative experiences, or from being born into a society which acknowledges homosexuality. See also **essentialism**.

social worker noun: a gay man who cruises around the homeless and unemployed, usually looking for **rough trade**.

soft butch noun: a masculine looking and acting lesbian but one who would be more willing to be receptive sexually, or has a gentler side.

some noun: sex. 'I gotta get me some or I'll go mad!'

son noun: a younger, usually submissive gay man who seeks a **daddy**.

SOS trip noun: a *Shopping and Other Sins* trip. Also *retail therapy* or to *go buy yourself a little happy (Will and Grace).*

spag-fag noun: a gay man who is sexually attracted to Italian men. Also *spag-hag* (for anyone who finds Italian men sexy).

Special K noun: the hallucinogenic drug *ketamine hydrochloride*. Originally used by vets in animal surgery, it is usually snorted but can also be smoked with tobacco and marijuana. Common effects include hallucinations, visual distortions, lost sense of time and identity, disorientation, amnesia, delirium, respiratory problems, flashbacks, possible catatonic syndrome and death by overdose. Also known as *breakfast cereal, ket, ketaject, ketalar, ketamine, new ecstasy, psychedelic heroin, super K, vitamin K*. See **k-hole**.

spit one out the window verb: to refuse to swallow semen after fellating a man.

spit roast noun: to be the passive partner in simultaneous oral and anal sex with two other men.

spleening verb: a (most likely apocryphal and dangerous) form of **fisting** which involves inserting a hand into the anus, fingering the base of the spine.

stache noun: a moustache.

stagefright noun: the inability to get an erection.

stag-hag noun: a person who likes the company of heterosexual men.

stats noun: statistics about a person such as age, height, weight, build, hair colour, penis size etc. Commonly used in internet chat rooms.

stealth mode noun: a **transgendered** person who lives full-time in their preferred gender and does not reveal their birth sex to anyone.

sticky eye contact noun: an intense form of eye contact between two strangers who find each other very attractive.

sticky rice queen noun: an Asian man who is attracted to other Asian men. Derogatory.

stippling verb: a form of appearance alteration used by some **drag kings** and **f-t-m transgendered** people whereby the illusion of a beard is created via dotting the chin with an eyebrow pencil.

stone butch noun: a masculine lesbian, who is sometimes mistaken for a man. In African-American slang, 'stone' means *very* e.g. 'I'm stone broke'. A stone butch may be *emotionally stone,* finding it difficult to acknowledge or express emotions, *sexually stone,* not liking to have her genitals touched for sex, or *physically stone,* not liking to be touched at all. An extremely stone butch would be a *granite butch.*

stone femme noun: 1. a **femme** lesbian who never tries to **flip** her **stone butch** partner. 2. a femme lesbian who does not like to be touched.

stone male noun: a man who is afraid of being penetrated anally and feels he is sexually superior to others, sometimes resulting in violence.

storyline noun: an interesting (although often negative) development in someone's life. Taken from the philosophy that life is a badly scripted daytime soap opera and therefore best viewed ironically: 'Jim's boyfriend dumped him for his brother again! He gets all the best storylines.'

straight adjective/noun: heterosexual. Originally US slang meaning socially acceptable, conventional, respectable or sober, not under the influence of drugs. Used to refer to heterosexuality since at least as early as the 1940s. Also *str8* (used on the internet).

straight-acting, SA adjective: masculine, generally used as a positive evaluation. From gay personal advert slang. Some people object to this word with its implication that *gay-acting* is effeminate, or that it is only straight men who are masculine, and that acting straight is somehow 'better'. Also *straight-appearing, straight-looking.*

strap on noun: a **dildo** that can be attached to the body like a penis. Also *snap on, snap on tool.*

stray noun: a heterosexual man who possesses qualities that make him appear like a gay man. A mixture of **straight** and **gay**. From mid-1990s UK media slang.

stud noun: 1. a very attractive man. 2. a butch lesbian.

sub, submissive adjective: someone who derives sexual enjoyment from being dominated in a **BDSM** context. Often used in personal advert or internet slang.

subspace noun: a detached state of consciousness felt by a **bottom** during a **scene** with a **top**.

suffrin' from the fever adjective: to be in need of sex.

sugar daddy noun: generally an older man who financially supports his partner. 'Honey, the only way you're going to live in one of those fancy uptown apartments is if you sweet-talk your way into a sugar daddy's wallet.'

swan noun: a **pre-op f-t-m transsexual**.

sweetie, sweetiedarling noun: a slightly patronizing term of address, derived in part from being used by the character Edina in the 1990s UK sitcom *Absolutely Fabulous*. Almost always pronounced as *sweedie.*

switch noun: someone who changes roles in **BDSM** or **D&S** roleplay. The word can refer to cases where a person can be a **top** or **bottom** with the same partner at different times. It can also be used in situations involving several partners where a person is exclusively dominant with one person and submissive with another. Finally, it can refer to a person who almost always takes one role, but will switch for certain people or on certain occasions. Also known as a *tween*.

T

tag hag noun: someone who likes to wear expensive designer clothing. Also *label queen*.

take the meat out verb: to expose the penis.

take the veil verb: to abandon a gay or lesbian lifestyle e.g. by getting married.

talent noun: the availability of attractive men in a place.

tandoori queen noun: a gay man who is attracted to Indian or Pakistani men. Derogatory.

tats noun: tattoos. Used in personal advertising slang.

T-bird noun: a woman who is sexually attracted to **transsexuals**. See **trannie chaser**.

tea noun: 1. US slang for **tea dance**. 2. In the 1990s the London Tourist Board sent American travel agencies leaflets containing the slogan 'If you think South Beach is the only place for Tea, Think Again.' South Beach is a gay resort near Miami and tea in this sense could be a sexual pick-up. It is possible that *tea* derives from the initial letter of **trade**.

tea-bag verb: the act of 'dipping' the testicles onto someone's face or forehead, usually while performing an erotic dance. Popularized via the film *Pecker* (1998). US. This word can also be referred to cases where it is performed at parties upon people who have passed out from drinking too much. In this case, each testicle is lowered onto a closed eye-socket and the penis is flopped along the length of the nose.

tea dance noun: an afternoon dance, usually held outdoors, and popular in gay resorts such as Fire Island and Provincetown.

tea-room, T-room noun: US slang for a public restroom used by men to have sex. Popularized in 1970 by Laud Humphreys in his ethnographic study *Tearoom Trade*. A *tea-room queen* is a gay man who tends to conduct most of his sex life in public restrooms. See also **the beats**, **biffy**, **cottage**.

tell the story verb: to tell the truth. 'So honeychile, I said to that closet-case, come on bitch, tell the story!' Also *call it out, pour the T(ruth)*. **Drag queen** slang.

T-fuck noun: sex with a **transvestite**. The other partner is called a *T-fucker*.

thank you for sharing vocative: sarcastic response to being on the receiving end of **TMI**.

that girl/guy noun: someone who makes an embarrassing show of him/herself in a bar or club, particularly when drunk and on the dance-floor. From the late 1960s US sitcom *That Girl*.

three gates of hell noun: in the sacred Hindi scripture *The Bhagavad Gita*, the three gates of hell are lust, anger and greed, leading to downfall (or bondage) of an individual. However, in gay slang, the three gates of hell are a variation on the **cock ring**. Three chrome rings are attached to a leather strap. The first ring is worn around the base of the scrotum, while the other two rings are worn around the shaft of the penis. A version of this device which contains five rings is known as the *five gates of hell.*

three gets (the) noun: someone who you wish to 'get home, get off and then get out'. Used to refer to a casual sexual partner. 'Kit's good for the three gets but not much else.'

threesome, threeway noun: sex between three people. See **oreo sex**.

throw shade verb: to give off **attitude**.

Thursday adjective: heterosexual. UK. See **Wednesday**.

tickle slut noun: a **bottom** who likes to be tickled.

time-waster noun: personal advertising slang, usually used in the phrase 'no time-wasters' referring to people who lie about themselves, don't turn up for dates etc.

tired adjective: boring, passé. 'I hate to be the one to break it to you, but that little "Me, myself and I" thing that you have going on became tired about five minutes before you started it.' Also *old.*

Titanic adjective: wonderful, incredible.

tit clamps noun: small clamps, affixed to the nipple area for sexual pleasure during **BDSM** roleplay. See also **tit torture**.

tit torture noun: rough or sadistic play of the nipples for sexual gratification.

TMI noun: acronym for *Too Much Information,* when a person **over-shares**. 'So we were just sitting there and he came out with all this stuff about how his baby-sitter used to abuse him. It was like, TMI!'

to die for adjective: something that is 'must-have' or impressive.

toilet slave noun: 1. someone in a **D&S** relationship who is ordered to clean or worship toilets. 2. a **bottom** with a fetish for serving a **top**'s toilet habits. 3. someone who wishes to roleplay as a toilet.

tomcat noun: a handsome or sexually aroused lesbian.

tongue verb: to lick, kiss or suck a part of someone's body in order to give them sexual pleasure. See also **rim, blow job, body worship**.

top noun: 1. one who is the inserter during anal intercourse. See **active**. 2. the dominant person or **master** in **BDSM** roleplay. See also **bottom**. Easton and Liszt in *The Topping Book* (1995: 5) define a *top* as referring to 'sadists, dominants, masters, mistresses, owners, trainers, teachers, daddies, mommies, interrogators and other active parties.' *Top* can also be used as a verb.

top drop noun: feelings of depression or inadequacy after playing a **top** in **BDSM** roleplay.

topping from the bottom verb: a sexual encounter where a **bottom** controls the action in some way. See also **bossy bottom**.

top's disease noun: a set of delusions held by some **tops** whose egos have become over-developed – for example, that they have the right to be dominant to all the **bottoms** they meet, or that they are infallible.

top surgery noun: an operation performed on a **f-t-m transsexual** which removes breast tissue and constructs a male chest.

tossed salad noun: the act of **rimming**.

tough trade noun: an attractive man who is difficult to get into bed.

tourist noun: someone who visits certain bars, clubs, internet chatrooms etc., in order to derive a prurient thrill or a 'laugh' from what they find there. Tourists may sometimes have more covert motives. Also *damn tourist*.

TPE noun: acronym for *Total Power Exchange,* referring to a relationship between two **lifestylers** in which the submissive surrenders all decisions to the dominant.

trade noun: male sex. *Trade,* which is broadly a euphemism for a casual sexual partner dates back to the eighteenth century UK, and has taken on several shades of meaning. Earlier, in the seventeenth century, *the trade* was used as slang to refer to prostitution, whereas, by the twentieth century, *trade* was used by the navy to refer to the submarine service. Contemporary gay usages imply a non homosexual pickup, or a homosexual prostitute: 'Today's trade is tomorrow's competition'. The word can also be used collectively, to refer to male prostitutes or to gay men as a group. *Trade* can also be used to refer to body fluids produced as a result of gay sex: 'I was so surprised I almost coughed up last night's trade.'

Tragicula noun: a nickname for someone who's had a tragic life, or has poor fashion sense.

trannie, tranny noun: a **transvestite**. Also *transie*.

trannie chaser noun: 1. anyone with a fetish for **transgendered** people. 2. males who are enamoured of **m-t-f cross-dressers** and **transsexuals**. Also *trans catcher, transfan, tranny hawk*.

transfag noun: a person who is both gay and **f-t-m transsexual**. Also *FTG* (female to gay). See **tryke**.

transgender noun: a term which covers anyone who challenges stereotypically gender boundaries or enjoys or needs to express an opposite sex identity e.g. **drag queen**, **drag king**, **female impersonator**, **hermaphrodite**, **transsexual**, **transvestite**. Also *cross-wired*.

trans hag noun: someone who is attracted to **transgendered** people. See **drag hag**.

transition noun: the period of time during which a **transsexual** changes from one gender role to another.

transsexual noun: a person who believes that they are the opposite sex to that of their body and may receive gender realignment surgery. It's estimated that 1 in every 30,000 men and 2 in every 100,000 women are transsexual. Also *TS*. See **post-op transsexual**, **pre-op transsexual**.

transvestite noun: a person (usually a heterosexual male) who finds emotional and/or sexual gratification when wearing women's clothing. Some transvestites are sexually aroused by the clothes themselves. If is estimated that 2–3 per cent of men cross-dress. Also **trannie**, *TV*.

tribadism noun: 1. lesbianism. 2. specifically a sexual activity where one woman rubs another's pudenda with her thigh or a dildo.

trick noun: 1. a sexual pick-up. verb: 2. to pick someone up. Originally from 1920s US prostitute's slang 'to turn a trick', to perform a sexual act with a casual partner for money.

trick out verb: to have sex with someone else while you're in a committed relationship.

trick towel noun: a towel worn in **gay saunas** or **bathhouses**, in order to cover the genitals and wipe off **cum**.

troll 1. noun: an unattractive, old man, particularly one who won't take no for an answer. 2. verb: to walk around (see **Polari** entry for more details).

trolley dolly noun: a gay flight attendant. Also *cart tart*.

tryke noun: a **m-t-f transsexual** who is also a lesbian. Also *female lesbian, transdyke*. See **transfag**.

tuck verb: to hide the penis in a skimpy outfit. **Drag queen** slang, quoted in Darrin Hagen's *The Edmonton Queen* (1997).

tuna noun: used by gay men to refer to a woman's vagina. Derogatory. Also *smell her*!

twink a young, attractive gay man, usually with little or no body hair and not incredibly intelligent. The stereotypical standard of westernized gay male beauty. US.

twink code noun: a classificatory system, derived from the **bear code**, used for identifying different types of

twinks. The code consists of the letter T followed by a number from 1 to 10, indicating the 'style' of twink: 1. Beach, 2. Nuevo-west, 3. Rap, 4. All-American, 5. Euro, 6. Twink Next Door, 7. Radical, 8. Gym, 9. Appalachian, 10. Grunge. This is followed by the letter C (hair colour) and a number from 0 to 9 where 0 = black hair and 9 = totally blonde. Next is the letter L (hair length) and a number from 0 to 6 where 0 = shaved or bald and 6 = very long. Other letters can be added (with positive and minus signs to indicate the extent to which a twink possesses a particular trait) such as h (hairlessness), d (dizziness), a (attitude), w ('whine' factor) c (colour of 'crust' or tan), y (youthful appearance), e (endowment or penis size), g (size of gonads), f (flavour of semen: sweet or bitter), t (preference for sex with other twinks), k (kinky factor), s (slut factor), m (muscularity), q (queeniness or effeminacy). So Dawson from *Dawson's Creek* could be classed as T4 C8 L3 a+ w c y+ k- s- q-.

twinkle toes noun: a young, effeminate gay man.

twirled adjective: 1. hyperactive, wired. 2. under the influence of drugs.

TWRL noun: acronym for *Those Who Refuse Labels* – people who refuse to be categorized according to gender, sex or sexuality.

U

über gay adjective: very gay.

U-haul noun: a lesbian who tends to fall in love and move in very quickly with her partner. 'What does a lesbian take on her second date?' 'A U-haul.'

uncut, u/c adjective: uncircumcized. Also *blind, near-sighted, skin queen, turtleneck.*

undercover adjective: to be **cross-dressed**.

uptown white woman noun: an extravagant, glamorous woman (of any colour).

Urning noun: a homosexual man. Coined by Karl Heinrich Ulrichs in his 1864 pamphlet *Vindex*. According to Ulrichs, Urnings were attracted to men because they were apparently hermaphrodites of the mind.

ursine adjective: looking like a **bear**.

ursophile noun: a young, slender man with no body hair who is attracted to **bears**.

usual damage noun: the same old story, nothing's changed. US slang.

V

vampire run: noun: cruising for sex in the early hours of the morning.

vanilla noun: conventional sex. 'It could never work out between us, I'm a vanilla queen and you're into pig sex and watersports!' It is generally believed that this word originates from the plain flavour of vanilla ice-cream, but it may also be derived from techno slang where a *vanilla personal computer* is one which is very basic. Also *in-and-out, regular trick.*

vanity smurf noun: a gay man who continually looks at his reflection in a mirror. Common among **muscle Marys** who like to stare at themselves in the wall-to-wall mirrors at the gym.

vegetarian noun: a gay man who will not give oral sex.

Vera noun: vomit. From **Gayle**.

verbal abuse, VA noun: hurtful insults given from a **top** to a **bottom** during **BDSM** or **D&S** roleplay, in order to push the bottom into **subspace**.

versatile adjective: to be comfortable being **passive** or **active** sexually.

very adjective: with-it, fashionable, up-to-date. 'Oh he's very!'

VGL adjective: personal advert acronym for *Very Good Looking*.

vibrator noun: an electrical device which vibrates. Unlike **dildos**, vibrators don't always tend to be exact representations of a penis and are not always used for anal or vaginal penetration – they can also be used to stimulate the penis, scrotum, nipples, clitoris and vulva.

vogue noun: a form of dance, popularized by Madonna in 1990 which consists of lots of stylized poses, similar to those used by a fashion model on a catwalk. Derived from the fashion magazine of the same title.

vulvaphobia noun: a fear, hatred or disgust of female genitals.

VWE adjective: personal advert acronym for *Very Well Endowed*. Also *XWE* – extremely well endowed. See **well-hung**.

W

waist cincher noun: an undergarment made of elastic which holds in the stomach, creating a slimmer waistline, used by male **cross-dressers**.

wank buddy noun: someone to meet for the purposes of mutual masturbation, with no other sexual contact taking place. UK.

wannabe noun: a heterosexual man who displays curiosity about the gay scene and may eventually go **on the turn**. In mainstream slang this word usually refers to someone who is desperate to become famous.

wannabe breeder noun: gay men or lesbians who lead a double life with an opposite sex partner. Derogatory. See also **beard, breeder, closet case**.

wash and go verb: to have sex with someone and then immediately leave.

watch queen noun: 1. someone who derives pleasure from voyeurism. Also *eyeball queen, peek freak*. 2. someone who acts as a lookout in a **cottage** (see **Polari** entry) or **tea room**.

water chestnut noun: a gay Japanese man.

watersports, WS noun: sex involving urine. This can involve **golden showers**, or other activities such as ingestion of urine, wetting one's pants (or ordering someone to wet theirs), or having the bladder controlled either through verbal commands, or by devices which cause or prevent urination. Also *mundo liquids*.

wave the rainbow verb: to sound off about issues surrounding gay and lesbian equality. See **rainbow flag**.

wedding ring noun: a ring, usually worn on the ring-finger of the right hand by gay men, either to signify that they are gay, or that they are in a long-term relationship. See also **pinky ring**.

Wednesday adjective: gay. UK. See **Thursday**.

weekend warrior noun: someone who lives a gay lifestyle at weekends, but is closeted during the rest of the week.

WEHO noun: West Hollywood, California.

well-hung adjective: possessing a large penis. Also *baby's arm, beer can, big bird, big brother, donkey dong, horsecock, horsemeat, jaw-breaker, kidney-buster, shoe shop, swanksa, tons of meat, VWE, WE, XWE.*

wet and messy noun: a sexual fetish involving having one's clothes or body covered in wet, messy substances such as mud, oil, honey, chocolate syrup, ice cream or body wastes.

whoops! vocative: to exclaim to friends that a gay man has been recognized.

widow (the) noun: someone whose lovers don't last for longer than a week.

wig out verb: to have a good time.

willing for a shilling adjective: sexually available. UK slang.

winkle noun: a small penis. Also *agate, chicken-wing, dink, gnat meat, hung like a tictac, love dart, narrow at the equator, needle dick, pea in the pocket, pee-pee meat, pee-wee, pencil dick, tiddler*.

witch noun: an ugly, unpleasant or old gay man, especially one who appears to have magical powers e.g. he's mysteriously able to attract good-looking men or has unusual insight in some way.

with it vocative: the equivalent of saying 'yes'.

WLTM acronym: advertising slang for *Would Like To Meet*.

wolf noun: 1. an **otter** who is sexually aggressive. **Bear** slang. 2. any gay man with a high sex drive. 3. an aggressive lesbian.

woman noun: an effeminate gay man.

woof vocative: used to signal that you find someone sexy. Derived from **bear** slang. An attractive bear would be *woofy*.

woozie noun: someone who has been **cruising** you or one of your group. US.

work verb: to network, while having an agenda.

worked adjective: riled, annoyed. A shortened version of 'worked up'

work it! 1. vocative: a **drag queen** phrase of support or encouragement, similar to **go girl!** 2. verb: to show off or flaunt something.

wrinkle queen noun: one who likes to have sex with very old men.

WTW noun: a term used in the porn industry to describe women who have sex with women but do not identify as lesbians. See **gay for pay**, **MSM**.

X

X queen noun: a gay man who often takes Ecstasy.

Y

yoo-hoo! vocative: an attempt by the UK gay radio station *LBH* to parody the Budweiser 'Whassssup!' advert – *yoo-hoo*! being ironically touted as the 'gay' equivalent of 'Whassssup!'

yosie noun: someone who is inexperienced at gay sex.

you better vocative: a way of returning a compliment. If someone says 'you're so pretty/good at dancing etc.' the response would be 'you better'.

yum-yuk noun: a person who you are both attracted to and repulsed by at the same time.

Z

zap action noun: a loud, showy type of **direct action** which would attract the attention of the media.

zombie noun: someone whose sexual partner has just ejaculated into their eyes, rendering them temporarily blind.

zsa-zsa verb: to slap someone. Named after Zsa-Zsa Gabor who is famously said to have slapped a traffic cop.

?VE adjective: unsure of **HIV** status. Used in personal advertising slang.

+VE adjective: **HIV** positive. Used in personal advertising slang. HIV negative is *–VE.*

12 o'clock preposition: straight ahead. 'Check out the hottie at 12 o'clock!'

123 words (the) noun: the US armed forces policy which prohibited gay men and lesbians from serving in the military between 1981 and 1993. See **don't ask, don't tell**.

24/7 noun: twenty-four hours a day, seven days a week. Can be used to refer to a consensual **BDSM** relationship. See **lifestyler, slave contract**.

24 hour girl noun: a drag queen who's a 'girl' all the time.

3 o'clock preposition: to the right.

4-real adjective: someone who is 'genuine' – not interested in one-night-stands or people who lie or exaggerate.

411 noun: information about someone, from the US telephone directory assistance number. 'Ask Marty, he's got the 411 on him.'

4:20 adjective: pot (marijuana) friendly. Advertising slang.

429 adjective: gay. Spells G-A-Y on a touch-tone telephone. The opposite, *924* means straight. From *The Broken Hearts Club* (2000).

9 o'clock preposition: to the left.

REFERENCES

Adams, H. E., Wright, L. W. and Lohr, B. A. (1996) 'Is Homophobia Associated with Homosexual Arousal?', *Journal of Abnormal Psycology*, 105, pp. 440–5.

Allen, L. S. and Gorski R. A. (1992) 'Sexual orientation and the size of the anterior commissure in the human brain', *Proceedings of the National Academy of Sciences of the USA*, vol. 89, pp. 7199–202.

Badgett, M. L. V. (2001) *Money, Myths and Change – The Economic Lives of Lesbians and Gay Men*. Chicago: University of Chicago Press.

Bornstein, K. (1998) *My Gender Workbook*. New York: Routledge.

Butler, J. (1990) *Gender Trouble: Feminism and the Subversion of Identity*. New York: Routledge.

Carpenter, E. (1895) *Homogenic Love and its Place in a Free Society*. Manchester: Manchester Labour Press.

Coates, J. (1993) *Women, Men and Language*. London: Longman.

Cory, D. W. (1967) 'The Language of the Homosexual', *Sexology 32.3*, pp. 163–5.

Crisp, Q. (1968) *The Naked Civil Servant*. London: Jonathan Cape.

Davidson, M. (1962) *The World, The Flesh and Myself*. London: A. Barker.

Davies, R. (1994) *The Kenneth Williams Diaries*. London: HarperCollins.

Easton, D. and Liszt, C. A. (1995) *The Topping Book*. San Francisco: Greenery Press.

Easton, D. and Liszt, C. A. (1997) *The Ethical Slut: A Guide To Infinite Sexual Possibilities*. San Francisco: Greenery Press.

Foote, S. (1753) *The Englishman in Paris. A Comedy in Two Acts (and in Prose)*. London.

Gardiner, J. (1997) *Who's A Pretty Boy Then? One Hundred and Fifty Years of Gay Life in Pictures*. London: Serpent's Tail.

Gibbs, R. W. and Nagaoka, A. (1985) 'Getting the hang of American slang: Studies on understanding and remembering slang metaphors', *Language and Speech*, 26: Part 2, pp. 177–95.

Grahn, J. (1990) *Another Mother Tongue*. Boston: Beacon Press.

Hagen, D. (1997) *The Edmonton Queen*, Edmonton, Alta: Slipstream Books.

Hamer, D. H., Hu, S., Magnuson, V. L., Hu, N. and Pattatucci, A. M. L. (1993) 'A Linkage Between DNA Markers on the X Chromosome and Male Sexual Orientation', *Science 261*, pp. 321–7.

Herek, G. M. and Capitanio, J. P. (1996) '"Some of my best friends": Intergroup contact, concealable stigma, and heterosexuals' attitudes toward gay men and lesbians', *Personality and Social Psychology Bulletin, 22*, pp. 412–24.

Humm, M. (1989) *The Dictionary of Feminist Theory*. Hemel Hempstead: Harvester Wheatsheaf.

Humphreys, L. (1970) *Tearoom Trade*. London: Duckworth.

Innes, S. A. and Lloyd, M. E. (1996) 'G.I. Joes in Barbie Land: recontextualizing butch in twentieth-century lesbian culture', in Beemyn, B. and Eliason, M. (eds), *Queer Studies: A Lesbian, Gay, Bisexual and Transgender Anthology*. New York: New York University Press, pp. 9–34.

Kinsey, A. (1948) *Sexual Behaviour in the Human Male*. Philadelphia: Saunders.

Kramer, L. (1978) *Faggots*. London: Minerva.

Legman, G. (1941) 'The Language of Homosexuality: An American Glossary.' In Henry, G. (ed.) *Sex Variants: A Study of Homosexual Patterns*. New York: P. B. Hoeber Inc., pp. 1147–78.

LeVay, S. (1991) 'A difference in hypothalamic structure between heterosexual and homosexual men', *Science 253*, pp. 1034–7.

Long, S. (1993) 'The Loneliness of Camp', in Bergman, D. (ed.) *Camp Grounds*. Massachusetts: Massachusetts Press, pp. 78–91.

Luirink, B. (2000) *Moffies*. Cape Town: David Philip.

Maupin, A. (1980) *More Tales of The City*. New York: Harper Collins.

Medhurst, A. (1997) 'Camp', in Medhurst, A. and Munt, S. R. (eds) *Lesbian and Gay Studies: A Critical Introduction*. London: Cassell, pp. 274–93.

Meyer, M. (ed.) (1994) *The Politics and Poetics of Camp*. London: Routledge.

OED (1994) *Oxford English Dictionary on CD-Rom* (2nd Edn.). Oxford: Oxford University Press.

Partridge, E. (1970) *Slang, Today and Yesterday*. London: Routledge.

Rice, G., Anderson, C., Risch, N. and Eber, G. (1999) 'Male homosexuality: absence of linkage to microsatellite markers at Xq28', *Science 284*, 665–7.

Rodgers, B. (1972) *The Queen's Vernacular*. San Francisco: Straight Arrow Books.

Ross, A. (1993) 'Uses of Camp', in Bergman, D. (ed.) *Camp Grounds*. Massachusetts: Massachusetts Press, pp. 54–77.

Ross, A. (1989) *No Respect, Intellectuals and Popular Culture*, New York: Routledge.

Rutledge, L. (1996) *The New Gay Book of Lists*. Boston: Alyson.

Sedgwick, E. K. (1991) *Epistemology of the Closet*. Hemel Hempstead: Harvester Wheatsheaf.

Simpson, M. (ed.) (1996) *Anti-gay*. London: Freedom Editions.

Sontag, S. (1966) 'Notes on Camp' in *Susan Sontag Against Interpretation and Other Essays*. New York: Farrarr, Straus, & Giroux, pp. 275–92.

Weinberg, G. (1972) *Society and the Healthy Homosexual*. Boston: Alyson.

Zipf, G. K. (1935) *The Psycho-Biology of Language*. Boston: Houghton Mifflin.

INDEX